Francis & Edith
Schaeffer

WOMEN OF FAITH SERIES

Amy Carmichael
Corrie ten Boom
Florence Nightingale
Gladys Aylward

Hannah Whitall Smith
Isobel Kuhn
Joni
Mary Slessor

MEN OF FAITH SERIES

Andrew Murray
Borden of Yale
Brother Andrew
C. S. Lewis
Charles Colson
Charles Finney
Charles Spurgeon
D. L. Moody
Eric Liddell
George Muller
Hudson Taylor
Jim Elliot

Jonathan Goforth
John Hyde
John Newton
John Paton
John Wesley
Luis Palau
Martin Luther
Samuel Morris
Terry Waite
William Booth
William Carey

John and Betty Stam
Francis and Edith Schaeffer

WOMEN & MEN OF FAITH

Francis & Edith
Schaeffer

L.G. Parkhurst, Jr.

BETHANY HOUSE PUBLISHERS
MINNEAPOLIS, MINNESOTA 55438

Published by Bethany House Publishers
A Ministry of Bethany Fellowship, Inc.
11300 Hampshire Avenue South
Minneapolis, Minnesota 55438

Printed in the United States of America.

**Library of Congress Cataloging-in-Publication
Data**

Parkhurst, Louis Gifford, 1946–
    Francis and Edith Schaeffer / L. G. Parkhurst, Jr.
       p. cm. — (Women and men of faith)

    1. Schaeffer, Francis A. (Francis August)
2. Schaeffer, Edith. 3. L'Abri (Organization)—
Biography. 4. Christian biography—United States.
5. Christian biography—Switzerland. I. Title.
II. Series.
BV4406.8.P37   1996
267'.13'0922—dc20
[B]   96–4502
ISBN 1–55661–843–3   CIP

Francis and Edith Schaeffer
Founders of L'Abri Fellowship
The story of a family who helped others
find God high in the Swiss Alps.

L. G. PARKHURST, JR. is the author of two works on Francis Schaeffer and the compiler and editor of Edith Schaeffer's *The Art of Life*. He is also the author and editor of many other books on prayer and the devotional life and is the pastor of Bethel Congregational Church in Edmond, Oklahoma.

Contents

Introduction

F rancis and Edith Schaeffer founded L'Abri Fellowship in 1955 to show that God exists. They wanted to demonstrate to others the character and reality of God by the way they lived, taught, and prayed. L'Abri, which means "the shelter," was started in the French-speaking part of Switzerland. It became a refuge and study center for people seeking to understand the meaning of life. Thousands of young people from around the world streamed to the Schaeffers' chalet in the small village of Huémoz*, high in the Swiss Alps, because someone told them that Dr. Schaeffer could help them. L'Abri became an international study center, where people from many countries and the major religions met and talked about God, philosophy, and religion.

After professors and pastors learned the Schaeffers helped college students, some of them went to L'Abri. Many of these older people had been confused about God and life since their days in college. Some joined with the college-aged students and stayed at L'Abri for several months to study. One

---

* Pronounced "way-mow" or wā-mō.

9

pastor said, "Within thirty minutes of talking to Dr. Schaeffer, I knew he could answer all my major questions. Questions I had from my seminary days. I stayed until I got my answers."

So many came to L'Abri that the Schaeffers needed more people to help. Some of those who stayed to study eventually joined L'Abri and gave individual attention to the new arrivals. As more people sought and found answers, L'Abri grew and founded study centers in other countries.[1]

L'Abri helped so many people because the Schaeffers built it on prayer, and thus proved on a daily basis that God exists. People could see God in operation in their home and in the lives of those around them. The Schaeffers *prayed* for God to send the people of His choice to them; they *prayed* for God to send the money they needed without soliciting funds; they *prayed* for God to give them His direct leading and plan; and they *prayed* for God to send them co-workers of His choice.[2] Through daily prayer and God's provision in answer to prayer, they showed God's presence to those around them, especially to unbelievers. When God answered prayer, He proved His loving character and faithfulness. Through His answers to prayer, God showed that He deserves our love and service. When God answered their prayers, He proved the significance of His promises in the Bible.

Time magazine labeled Francis Schaeffer "the missionary to intellectuals." This label set him apart from all others. Schaeffer had to learn the language of philosophy and understand cultures from around the world in order to help searching young people who came to him from almost every nation on earth. Francis and Edith reasoned with people about God's existence, and also lived every day on the basis of God's being in daily communication with them. They strived to maintain a careful balance between the intellectual and the devotional life.[3] If you study their books and lives together, you will find good and sufficient reasons to believe in God and bow before Jesus Christ as your Lord and Savior. By the grace of God, their work proves the transforming power of the Word of Truth and the Holy Spirit. They showed that God loves to lead sinners to the Savior, and the Holy Spirit helps Christians live in faithful obedience.

A. W. Tozer wrote: "Next to the Holy Scriptures, the greatest aid to the life of faith may be Christian biography. It is indeed notable that a large part of the Bible itself is given over to the life and labors of prophets, patriarchs and kings—who they were, what they did and said, how they prayed and toiled and suffered and triumphed at last!"[4] In this biography of the Schaeffers, based in large part on their many books, God's marvelous and gracious intervention is shown in their lives. You will see that God exists, and will discover some principles upon which He acts in believers' lives.

God blessed the Schaeffers' efforts, and they began writing books in the 1960s. Because Dr. Francis Schaeffer's books circulated in several foreign languages, many people associate their work only with logical arguments for God's existence, with honest answers to honest questions, and with good reasons to be a Christian. However, time and again Dr. Schaeffer said that his books did not stand alone: his books stood with the books of his wife. Francis felt that to get a full understanding of L'Abri, people needed to read Edith's books as well.

Edith Schaeffer's books show the existence of God through answers to prayer and transformed lives. Her books give practical answers to everyday problems, and include *L'Abri; Common Sense Christian Living; What Is a Family?; Affliction; Christianity Is Jewish; Lifelines; The Art of Life; Forever Music; Everybody Can Know*; and *The Tapestry*. She wrote about their founding of L'Abri; how they based all their work on prayer and showed God's answers.

As you learn about how God prepared the Schaeffers for ministry, marvel at two things God placed on Edith's heart. These two things, which she thought would help *only one person and a few close friends*, made their work spread beyond Switzerland and still speak to us today. First, after they moved to Switzerland, God inspired Edith to write detailed letters home to her mother in America. These letters described God's day-to-day working in their lives, their work, some ways God answered their prayers, and some ways God bestowed grace in their afflictions and overcame Satan's attacks. Second, Edith wrote these letters in ways that would enable her mother to see things through her eyes. She filled her letters with life and vitality, and eventually carried this God-given talent and concern for others into her books. By inspiring her to write these long letters in the way she did, God taught her to write books in a way that would interest and involve thousands of readers for many years. God's guiding Edith to write her mother preserved for us a record that glorifies God.[5]

Dr. Schaeffer believed that a transformed life was one of the best arguments for God's existence. He prayed that God would help him show others by the way he lived the love of God and the truth of God *at the same time* in the power of the Holy Spirit.[6] Because I have known the Schaeffers since 1978 (and saw how they handled Dr. Schaeffer's terminal cancer for almost six years), and because I personally know how Edith has continued their ministry for twelve years since Francis's death, I can testify that they have been and are consistent, honest witnesses to the transforming truth, power, and love of God in the best, worst, and most difficult of times.[7] Edith prays that as a Christian she will be like solid wood all the way through, and not like pressed wood with veneer on top hiding what is underneath. Without hypocrisy, the Schaeffers have lived lives worthy of a Christian biography.

Because Francis and Edith Schaeffer decided to show others by the way they lived and taught that God exists, He gave them an exciting life. Described another way, because God wanted to show what He is like, He called the Schaeffers to begin L'Abri Fellowship and gave them many adventures. L'Abri became (and still is) a shelter for young people searching for answers to tough questions about life, God, and the way God works. God revealed His purpose to the Schaeffers as they prayed, studied the Bible, and talked together. Then they began L'Abri to show others that God is infinite, personal, powerful, loving, and holy. By their lives, they wanted to show the value of trusting in Jesus, the Son of God, and to show that God exists and what He is like by His working through them. This biography shows some events in which God revealed himself through them to others.

Hardships and persecution also motivated the Schaeffers to start L'Abri. So their story shows how

God can get people through tough situations and help them accomplish great things. The adversities they faced and overcame with God's help demonstrate the power of the Holy Spirit and show how He works through faith.

God did not only teach Francis and Edith how to debate to prove that He exists. Though Francis was an experienced debater, God and the Schaeffers chose a better way to win people for Jesus Christ. They proved that God is there by showing how He works in the world. Through the story of their lives, you will see how God can work in anyone's life. You will discover that God is not silent in the Bible or in today's world. God has spoken and made promises that He intends to keep now and forever. Through Francis Schaeffer's books, especially *The God Who Is There* and *He Is There and He Is Not Silent*, you will find answers to many questions and good reasons to believe in God. By looking at the lives of Francis and Edith Schaeffer, God will give you a glimpse of His work in the twentieth century. God shows through them that He is just as faithful and loving today as He was in Bible times.

Through their lives, God demonstrates the value of living on the basis of His promise: "In all thy ways acknowledge him, and he shall direct thy paths" (Proverbs 3:6, KJV). God visibly directed the work of Francis and Edith Schaeffer, because they chose to live according to His promises and commands in the Bible. They bowed before Jesus as their Lord and Savior, and looked to the Holy Spirit to empower them. They acknowledged God in everything they did, and He showed himself faithful through them. They studied their Bibles and intended to obey God's Word; therefore, the Holy

Spirit led them to understand and apply the spirit of God's Law as they made decisions. They tried to pray almost without ceasing, so they could recognize the leading of Jesus and stay close to Him as He led the way.

Biographies of Christians—of preachers, missionaries, writers, business people, statesmen, and theologians—teach us about God and what He can do through people dedicated to Him. They encourage us to draw closer to God, to pray, read the Bible, and seek to obey God. God began L'Abri in 1955, but before that could happen He brought two people—unlikely to be joined—together.

1

In Search of Answers

God worked a miracle when He brought Francis and Edith Schaeffer together, because their parents had raised them with such opposite values. Only God could prepare them to accept and love each other. Despite their different experiences and education, God blended them into a couple and enabled them to help troubled people from all over the world.

Francis Schaeffer's great-grandfather "Franz" and his wife, Carolina, emigrated from Germany to the United States in 1869 to escape European wars, hardship, poverty, and famine. Franz came to work on the railroads, which hired thousands of Chinese and European immigrants. The same year they arrived in America, rail workers completed the world's first transcontinental railroad and linked the East and West Coasts. Joining many others from their homeland, the Schaeffers settled in Germantown, now a colorful neighborhood in northwest Philadelphia, Pennsylvania. The historic steam locomotive *Old Ironsides* made its first run through Germantown in 1832, and the expanding nation needed many young men to lay more railroad track, build steam engines, and switch cars in

17

the train yards. Franz worked in these busy train yards. Coal-burning locomotives made his work dirty, exhausting, and dangerous. Many men worked too hard and took risks, hoping for promotion to conductors and engineers someday.

In 1876, seven years after the Schaeffers came to America, Carolina gave birth to their only son, Francis August Schaeffer III. Sadly, just three years after Francis's birth, a railroad accident killed Franz. The burden of supporting the family fell on Carolina, so at a very early age Frank dropped out of school and went to work full time. His early childhood hardships influenced him to reject the Lutheran church and all ministers. They did not reach out and help the needy as he thought they should. The church seemed to be only for the rich, and pastors did not know how to work. Christianity for young Frank was worthless.

Frank married Bessie Williamson, who was also from Germantown. Bessie's grandfather, William Joyce, came to America from England and settled in Germantown in 1846. Her mother, Mary Joyce, married Wallace Williamson in 1877. Ten years later, when Bessie's father died, her mother had to care for her four children and an elderly father all by herself. Bessie experienced childhood hardships similar to those of Frank. They had to turn their home into a laundry to care for the family. Bessie became angry and bitter from the experience of helping her mother long hours each day. She hated the washing and ironing and caring for a large household. She recalled her childhood with pain. Though she attended the Evangelical Free Church and worked in Christian Endeavor, she refused to accept the Gospel or allow Jesus Christ to transform her bitter selfishness with His loving presence.

When Bessie was thirty-two years old, she gave birth to her only child, Francis August Schaeffer IV. Fran was born on January 30, 1912, in his parents' home on Pastoria Street, Germantown, Pennsylvania. Remembering her own difficult childhood, Bessie resolved to have only one child. Because of their German and English backgrounds, Fran's parents had received some religious training as a part of their culture, but they turned from this and gave little thought to raising Fran in a Christian home. After God called Fran to be a minister, they told him bluntly they did not want any son of theirs to be a pastor.

Fran developed an appreciation for the sacrifices and the spiritual values of America's founders from exploring and hiking around their historic neighborhood. German Mennonites under the leadership of Francis Daniel Pastorius founded Germantown in 1683. The first paper mill in the colonies was built there in 1690. During the Revolutionary War, General Howe defeated General George Washington and the colonial army in Germantown on October 4, 1777. Later, in 1793 and 1794, President George Washington claimed this town as his summer home.

As Frank and Bessie raised Fran, they expected him to follow in his father's footsteps and work honestly with his hands. They did not respect ministers, and they had never seen the Christian faith make any positive difference in anyone's life. Fran's father was hardworking and taught his son responsibility, the importance of manual labor, and the necessity of caring for one's family no matter what the personal sacrifice. Raised in a blue-collar home, Fran never looked down upon working in the trades or in any other honest industry. As he learned the trades, he came to appreciate the value of all types of work from his hardworking father. Later, as a minister, he lifted up hard, physical labor and working with your hands as the calling of God, just as much as some might be called to the intellectual labor of the pastor, teacher, or missionary. Many times he said, "The call to the ministry is no higher calling than any other." Each person is responsible before God to do His will in whatever vocation or profession God calls him to fulfill. Throughout his ministry, Fran cared for all unbelievers, because he had been raised by unbelievers to be an unbeliever.

Together, Frank and Bessie Schaeffer raised a healthy, strong, active, intelligent boy, who loved life and enjoyed others. He made worthwhile friendships in the Boy Scout Troop that met in the local Presbyterian Church. Scouting had come to America from England, in 1910, so that churches could reach out to young boys, especially those who had no church home. In the early days, the Boy Scout Motto was "Be Prepared for the Second Coming of Christ." The Boy Scouts drew Fran into the church and Sunday school. However, because the preacher did not base his sermons on the Bible, Fran did not find them helpful. The honest believers in the church inspired Fran, and he appreciated what a church could do to help others.

Fran learned many important values from his unbelieving father: he learned to persevere and work hard, and the value of doing an honest day's labor for an honest day's wage. He saw that non-Christians could be "good people," even better than some who claimed to be Christians. This fact led to his eventual understanding that no one can earn salvation by their good works or by going to church. Fran came to realize that both believers and unbelievers can do many wonderful things, because God made people in His image with abilities that should be used for His glory and honor.

Fran's parents went to great lengths to plan his life for him. They spent whatever they could afford to give him opportunities they had not enjoyed in their own childhood. They took him to the beach in Atlantic City, New Jersey, and on other family outings. But Fran and his father found their main enjoyment from working hard together in the trades. They had no greater "fun" than working side by side, and Fran's father dreamed of his son becoming an engineer. They remodeled their home together, and Fran ran the electrical wiring. His parents determined that he would get a degree in engineering and design, and then go to work with his father. They wanted him to do something practical, and did not challenge Fran intellectually or show concern for his spiritual growth. Their values and vision did not extend beyond living and working for what this life can give. They just wanted Fran to support himself and his family materially with a higher standard of living than they had enjoyed. Yet everything Fran learned from working with his hands he would later use to repair and maintain his family's homes in America and Europe.

Because Fran was not raised as a Christian, he did not see much meaning to life. Though his school records showed he was highly intelligent, he simply did not apply himself to his studies. There was no compelling reason to work hard or strive for excellence in his intellectual endeavors until after he came to faith in God: then he became a straight-A student. He attended Roosevelt Junior High School and Germantown High School, taking classes in the vocational and technical areas. Upon graduation, his parents planned for him to study engineering at Drexel Institute, so he prepared by taking courses in mechanical drawing, woodworking, metalwork, electrical design, and construction. By the time he graduated, he could lay flooring, build garages, lay brick, spread concrete, and do plumbing. During his high school years, he learned many practical skills that he would later use to overcome difficulties. He learned to be practical-minded and hard-working from his parents, and these values along with his early education would be absolutely essential after God led him to decide to live by faith as a missionary.

God began preparing Fran for the hard work of building L'Abri even as a child. L'Abri became "the shelter" in Europe and America for young people like Fran who did not know they were searching for God until they found Him. His work as a missionary would require much more than giving "honest answers to honest questions" around a cozy fire or writing books and making films: the things that made him famous. God prepared him, before he came to faith in Him, to do the hard and difficult manual and intellectual labor He had planned for him.

Unlike the home Fran eventually created for his own children, there were no philosophical or theological discussions or questions. His parents had no "love for wisdom," and they did not care to "reason about God." They had no concern for cultural things, and they knew nothing about what they were missing. Although they did not stimulate Fran's interest in the arts or music, Fran's interest grew during junior high school. He proved to be a capable public speaker, and at the age of eleven entered and won a speech contest sponsored by the Boy Scouts.

At the age of seventeen Fran began teaching English to a Russian immigrant. He needed to buy an English grammar book for him, so he went to the bookstore and found what he wanted. After he went home, he found they had wrapped up the wrong book and discovered instead that he had an introduction to Greek philosophy. The philosophy book interpreted life only from the human point of view. Its teachings relied on human reason alone and left many unanswered questions. But it grabbed Fran's interest and opened the door to intellectual pursuits.

Fran's studies in philosophy led him to discover the basic philosophical questions about the meaning of life. Seeking answers to these questions, he listened carefully to the preaching of his pastor. He did not find the answers from the sermons, for they only spoke about the necessity of doing good deeds. Fran later learned that the preacher taught from a liberal theological position, using ideas that had crept into many of the mainline protestant churches in the early 1900s. Such teaching was sometimes called "the social gospel." Liberal theology teaches that the Bible contains errors; therefore, God cannot be trusted to speak without making mistakes. Most liberal theologians deny many of the Bible's positive teachings about Jesus, including His Virgin Birth and miracles, the value of

His death on our behalf, and His Second Coming. They do not believe that everything Jesus said in the Bible is true. Theological liberals sometimes teach that God has never really spoken to people, and the Bible is nothing but people's thoughts and hopes about what God *might* be like. Before Fran knew what theological labels to use for different systems of thought, he learned that neither philosophy nor liberal theology could answer his questions or give meaning to life.

The book he unwrapped and read "by mistake" was not the Bible, because God knew which book Fran needed to read first in order to prepare him to study and understand the Bible. Fran needed to know the right questions, so he could later discover that the Bible had the right answers. But before Fran ever got to the Bible, he concluded that the Christianity he was learning at church could not answer the deep questions about life. Fran thought that perhaps he needed to be honest about his unbelief and quit going to church, like his father had done. But first he decided to be fair and read the Bible for himself. He began at the beginning and read straight through to the end. From reading Genesis to Revelation, he discovered that the Bible contained the answers to his philosophical questions. In the course of about six months, at the age of seventeen, the truth of God and the Spirit of God led Fran to become a Christian. However, he did not know anyone else who believed as he did.

Although filled with the excitement of a new and growing faith, Fran could not talk to his parents. They would not have understood how he could have moved from not knowing whether or not there was a God, to reading philosophy, to reading the Bible, and then to finding the very answers he sought. Later, when he tried to explain his faith to them, his ideas were dismissed without discussion. Fran observed, "What rang the bell for me was the answers in Genesis, and that with these you had answers—real answers—and without these there were no answers either in philosophy or in the religion I had heard preached."[1] Much later he wrote the book *Genesis in Space and Time* because of his firm belief that the first book of the Bible is the foundation that holds it all together and gives it meaning.

One hot August evening in 1930, out of curiosity and without knowing that God was leading him, Fran wandered into an old-fashioned tent-meeting revival. He walked down the aisle on the clean sawdust that the workers had sprinkled on the ground, and he quietly sat down on one of the creaky wooden folding chairs. The preacher on the raised wooden platform looked out at the people with piercing but kindly eyes as he spoke with enthusiasm. After his sermon, the preacher called for repentant sinners to come forward as the congregation sang old hymns and the pianist played.

For a hundred years in America, revivalists had traveled from town to town. They often raised a tent, led people in rousing songs, and preached so people would commit their lives without reservation to serving Jesus as their personal Lord and Savior. The revivalists hoped to bring dead churches back to life by inspiring Christians to do their duty. Revived Christians could then lead sinners to repent of their sins and turn to God. Revivalists also preached so sinners would "hit the sawdust trail" and come forward to a kneeling bench or rail. In front of the raised platform, they encouraged sinners to repent, pray, and give their lives to Jesus Christ.

Fran listened carefully to the man when he preached from the Bible. Fran had never heard such preaching before. Here was the real Gospel preached according to the Scriptures, just as he had learned from his own independent study. At the altar call, when the preacher asked people to come forward and give their lives to Christ, Fran went forward and took the side of God with those who believed in the God of the Bible.

Fran made his decision because Christianity is true, and later he decided that this is the *only* reason to become a Christian. Since the Bible's teachings are reasonable and true to life, they make sense. The Scriptures, grounded in God's acts in history and people's lives, give a logical presentation of the truth. People can talk about, explain, and share the reasonable system of Christian thought with others. The Bible contains the only answers to the meaning of life and the questions life poses. Later Fran wrote, "The basis for our faith is that certain things are true. The whole man, including the intellect, is to act upon the fact that certain things are true. That, of course, will lead to an experiential relationship with God, but the basis is content, not experience."[2]

While a teenager, Fran learned what he later preached often: the Bible is true in all that it affirms, and the Bible is God's revelation to save lost and dying people. Searching people discover the questions of life, and then they find that God has already thought of the questions and given the answers in the Bible. As a pastor and missionary,

Fran used these truths as strong arguments for the authority and reliability of the Bible as a revelation from God.

After the tent-meeting revival, Fran knew he had more choices to make. He had decided to believe in, trust, and obey Jesus Christ, rather than continue living his life on his own terms or according to other people's plans. When he accepted Jesus as his Savior, he also received Jesus as his Lord. God did not overpower him or program him to make him into a Christian. God did not force him to make a decision against his will. In spite of great struggles, Fran walked joyfully and willingly in the path God chose for him. God led Fran gently by the compelling truth of His Word, the Bible. He enlightened him by the power of the Holy Spirit, and Fran made an intelligent and responsible choice to follow Jesus wherever He might lead. Then Fran prayed for God to help him make all his future choices day by day. For these and other reasons, Fran never tried to manipulate others or stimulate them to make only an emotional decision to give their lives to God.

Though God prepared Fran for his life's work, He did so through the tough choices Fran made as he faced the challenges of reality and those who did not know God. Shortly after becoming a Christian, Fran experienced the Holy Spirit's call to the Christian ministry. As he felt the joy of that calling, he knew what a heartbreak this would be to his parents! He knew how antagonistic they would be. How could he convince his parents to accept this change of vocation, especially when they felt all ministers were little more than parasites upon society?

2

Do Opposites Attract?

God prepared Edith Rachel Merritt Seville to
work as a missionary by bringing her into a
world very different from Fran's. Her parents had the opposite outlook on the Christian faith
from Fran's parents. It is hard to imagine how dif-
ferently the two of them were raised, but God
blended these differences beautifully into an effective missionary couple, giving each one abilities
and backgrounds the other lacked so they could be
true partners.

Edith's parents were of Irish-English ancestry.
Her father's grandparents came to America from
Ireland in 1844 and settled in Pittsburgh, Pennsylvania. Her mother's ancestors came from England in the early 1800s, and settled first in Pennsylvania and then in Ohio. Her mother, Jessie
Maude Merritt, was born in 1874. She married Walter Greene, and they planned to serve in the China
Inland Mission, which J. Hudson Taylor had
founded in 1865. Taylor's books on faith and prayer
enkindled a desire in Walter and Jessie to join his
band of dedicated workers who dressed in Chinese
clothing and followed Chinese customs. Taylor inspired them to love China's millions and seek their

salvation. But in 1895, after one year of marriage, their first child died at birth. The little baby boy was strangled by his own cord as he came into the world. Then, three weeks later, Walter died of tuberculosis. Jessie lost her dearest earthly loves, but she did not lose her love for God and the Chinese people she and Walter had prayed they could serve. As a woman of courage and devotion, Jessie left on her own to attend Toronto Bible College and prepare for missionary work with the China Inland Mission. In spite of her afflictions, she completed her schooling and left for Shanghai, China, in 1899.

Edith's father, George Hugh Seville, was born in 1876. He loved to study languages, especially Greek and Hebrew. He graduated with the A.B. degree from Westminster College, New Wilmington, Pennsylvania, in 1898. For two years he taught Latin and Greek in a boy's prep school, but as he learned about and prayed for Hudson Taylor's China Inland Mission, God called him to the mission field. He attended a Presbyterian theological seminary for three years, where he received high marks in the study of Hebrew, and then sailed for China in late 1902. In China, George met Jessie Maude Merritt. Jessie had determined that she would never marry again. She did not think anyone could replace Walter, and she convinced herself that she could serve God better as a widow. She thought marriage and caring for children might interfere with her ability to serve the Chinese people without distraction. George persevered in pursuing her, and finally won her heart. They were married on March 29, 1905, the same year Hudson Taylor died.

George and Jessie began their family in China,

and their fourth child, Edith, was born on November 3, 1914. A precocious and strong-willed child, Edith spent her early life in the missionary compound of the China Inland Mission. She observed her parents' love for Christ and the Chinese people. She learned Chinese and appreciated the work of the China Inland Mission. Her parents taught her how to dress like Chinese children and encouraged her to love the little Chinese boys and girls around her. She even learned how to drink tea with rice packed in one cheek, not to be touched by the tea.

God's early preparation of Edith included having her accompany Dr. Hoste (who succeeded Hudson Taylor as the director of C.I.M.) as he prayed by name for all the missionaries under his care. After admonishing her not to talk as they walked, he took little four-year-old Edith by the hand as he prayed out loud for the mission's needs and the individual needs of each missionary and their children. Edith heard Dr. Hoste pray for her specifically, and then she saw his prayers answered on her behalf. She heard others praising God for the answers to prayer that she had heard Dr. Hoste pray about earlier, and she praised God too. Some of her earliest recollections include hearing her parents pray and seeing God answer them in special ways. Very early in life, God impressed Edith's heart and mind with truths about His faithfulness and His desire to hear and answer prayers.

In 1919 the Sevilles returned from China, and Edith's dad continued working with C.I.M. as editor of *China's Millions*. Later, he became the pastor of the Presbyterian Church in Newburgh, New York. He kept studying the Bible and theology, and maintained friendships with such great Christian leaders as Robert Dick Wilson and J. Gresham Machen, professors at Princeton Theological Seminary. The intellectual interests of Edith's father played an important role in her life, and while she was still in high school, her father gave her the books of these two great men to study so she could better prepare herself to defend the Christian faith.

After the Sevilles moved to Pennsylvania, Edith fought for the truth and defended the Christian faith in her high school classes and in church. Sometimes speakers in her church youth meetings denied Christian truth and the Bible's teachings, and Edith did not want others to be misled by false ideas. She loved to read the Bible and pray, and daily devotions became an integral part of her life. She learned to blend Bible reading and prayer together by praying over each verse of the Bible as she read.

While Edith attended high school and learned more about God from her parents, Fran faced hostile parents who opposed his plans for ministry. They fiercely resisted the idea, for they had planned for him to get a degree in engineering. He quickly discovered that he would need to go against his parents' wishes if he were to study and prepare for the ministry! He chose to obey God rather than man, but this meant real pain to himself and both of his parents. In his later ministry, he remembered what choosing to obey Christ could mean in the life of any young person he counseled. His mother carried an unforgiving bitterness far into his years of ministry, and in many ways made life miserable for the entire Schaeffer family as they cared for her in her declining years of life.

After some Christian friends and leaders in his

church advised him, Fran applied for admission to Hampden-Sydney College in Virginia. He thought it best to begin preministerial studies in the fall of 1931. He had no idea how he would finance his schooling, but he prayed and trusted that if the Lord had called him to the ministry, then the Lord would meet his needs.

While working and preparing for college, Fran studied Latin and German in night school. During the day he worked equally hard to earn money for school. He believed that God would provide for his needs as he prepared for the ministry, but he also knew that God expected him to work diligently to prepare himself in every way for his calling—materially, intellectually, and spiritually. Years later, students who came to L'Abri quickly learned that Dr. Schaeffer expected them to do both intellectual and physical labor as they grew spiritually.

In September 1931, Fran prepared to leave for college. A little more than a year had passed since he had publicly professed his faith in Jesus Christ as his Lord and Savior. He felt joyful about going to school where he could learn more about the way upon which he had embarked. But still he didn't have his father's blessing or permission. As an obedient son, he did not want to go against the wishes of his father. He felt torn between his obligations to his earthly father and to his heavenly Father. He sincerely felt a personal struggle between God's call to the ministry and his father's call to work beside him.

The day finally came when Fran had to leave for college. His dad met him at the door as he was going off to work and commanded his son directly: "I don't want a son who is a minister, and—I don't want you to go."[1] Fran told his dad to give him just a few more minutes to decide what to do. He went down to the cellar and prayed. He fervently sought the Lord's will once again, seeking a final confirmation that in this situation he *could* disobey his earthly father and prepare for ministry. Then, after God reaffirmed His will for him, Fran went upstairs to see his dad, who was waiting to hear his decision. Sorrowfully, and without a hint of rebellious spirit in his words, Fran said, "Dad, I've got to go. . . ."[2] With that, his father slammed the door in anger behind him . . . but he also called out that he would pay Fran's school expenses for the first half year.

Years later Fran's dad did become a Christian, but if Fran had not made the decision to follow his heavenly Father, no matter what the personal cost in family and friends, his own earthly father might never have found Christ as his Savior. Literally thousands of others might never have come to a deep Christian faith if Fran had not chosen at that one moment in history to put God first in his life no matter what the personal cost. The decisions we make *now* can cause ripple effects throughout eternity!

Fran's arrival at Hampden-Sydney was not easy. He came from a working-class home and worked as a low-paid, blue-collar worker. By contrast, his fellow students who came from the American aristocracy were rich, well-dressed, and often spoiled. He was a Northerner, a Yankee from Philadelphia, while they were Southern gentlemen. They gave him the nickname "Phily." They knew he was studying to be a minister, and many felt compelled to test that commitment. School authorities deliberately placed Fran on a dormitory floor with students who were especially belligerent toward ministerial students. In spite of this, Fran showed his strong religious convictions and refused to live hypocritically or compromise his beliefs. Fran had to demonstrate through his actions and study habits that he had a heartfelt concern for people. Over the next four years, they learned of Fran's convictions about God and what it meant to serve Him only, but at first, they did not want to be near a person who might bother their conscience as they threw off the religious morality of their home life.

While Fran stood for the holiness of God, he also needed to show the love of God and compassion for those who did not know the God of the Bible. At one point he made a pact with some students that if he helped them to their rooms after they came home on a Saturday night, they had to go to church with him on Sunday morning. He hoped they might hear and respond to the Gospel. He didn't mind this, and simply said, "It gave me time to keep up with my studies while the others were out." He started a prayer meeting and Bible study on his dorm floor, and many attended. To hold their interest, he kept it short. At graduation, the school honored him for being the most outstanding Christian on campus during his four years.

Fran met Edith Seville on June 26, 1932. He had finished his first year at Hampden-Sydney College and had returned home to work for the summer. One Sunday evening at the First Presbyterian Church, a Unitarian (who had been a member of the church) came to speak on why he denied the Bible's teachings regarding God, the deity of Jesus Christ, and other Christian truths. Following his talk, Edith had planned to argue against his ideas, using materials she had been studying. But before she could stand, Fran jumped up and began refuting what had just been said. Until that moment, Edith had not known of anyone else near her age in the church who believed as she did. When Fran finished speaking, Edith stood up and made her position clear. Fran did not know of anyone else in the church who believed as *he* did. That night, following the meeting, Francis Schaeffer insisted that he accompany Edith home. They had met on the field of spiritual combat, both fighting for the same biblical faith, both with intellectual passion. That night in June of 1932, God began a partnership of learning and teaching that would mark their work together.

While Fran finished the next three years at Hampden-Sydney College, they wrote each other every day. Their romance included sharing spiritual truths as well as personal truths. Edith encouraged Fran to read J. Gresham Machen's *Christianity and Liberalism*, and then they discussed the devastating effects theological liberalism was having on the church and some of those around them. For Fran and Edith, Christianity was never an intellectual theory or game. Even after Fran became a noted Christian thinker, he never just "theologized" for the sake of argument or discussion. He believed that theological discussion could become just another exciting game to some people, and that playing that game could actually become a barrier to real and honest discipleship.

During Fran's sophomore year at Hampden-Sydney, Edith began attending Beaver College for Women, commuting daily to save money. Their college years demonstrated their commitment to serving Christ. Consistent with his concern for all people, Fran walked through the woods every week to teach the Bible to a group of poor black children. He knew no barriers of race or color in Jesus Christ, and lived on that basis even when many had a deep-seated prejudice against their black brothers and sisters. Fran went to these little children because he loved them and saw them as individuals. But at the same time, perhaps unconsciously, he made a social statement regarding every Christian's responsibility to love and serve those who are different in some respects from themselves, for all human beings are created in the image of God. Among his other college activities, Fran became president of the Literary Society and entered debates. He served on the cabinet of the Christian Student Association and became a member of the Ministerial Association. He joined Theta Kappa Nu fraternity and fulfilled his obligations, but later he resolved never again to join another secular organization. He said that at some point secular, "this-world" organizations always come into conflict with the Christian faith and practice.

While Fran studied theology, Edith studied home economics, a wide and extensive curriculum, covering many different practical areas. Her Christian commitment led her to start meetings of the League of Evangelical Students on campus. These were also difficult times for her, as she had to face the challenges of those intellectuals who had embraced and were promoting communist positions regarding religion and social concerns. But God knew exactly what He was doing in preparing Edith for the mission field. She would help pay for Fran's seminary education by working as a seamstress.

Later, she would make clothes for herself and the children, and decorate their homes economically and beautifully.

Their correspondence during this time was full and rich. For example, Edith idealized that Fran would one day become a great man of God. She wanted to be his companion in *everything*. Fran remarked about the death of a fine professor and said that he would have been even greater "if he had had love in his life." At another time, they both rededicated their lives to God, to the point of being willing to part with each other if that were God's will for them. They both read *Daily Light* each day, to have a biblical and spiritual experience in common while apart. Their shared reading of *Daily Light* continued until the day of Fran's death.

In March of 1935, Fran applied for admission to theological seminary. As a straight-A student, he graduated magna cum laude and second in his class with a B.A. degree from Hampden-Sydney, so he could attend any seminary he chose. However, Fran and Edith did not find an easy glide from college to seminary because they were not isolated from the winds of change in their denomination. By April of 1935, Dr. J. Gresham Machen was on trial in the Presbyterian Church for his pioneering work in independent missions. Fran and Edith joined in prayer for him and their future. The result of that trial would affect their decision about whether or not to remain in the theologically liberal Presbyterian Church. When they learned that Dr. Machen had had his ordination credentials withdrawn, Fran wrote immediately and resigned from the Northern Presbyterian Church and went under care as a seminary student with the Presbytery of the Presbyterian Church of America.

Fran and Edith were partners in their decision to withdraw from the liberal Presbyterian Church. In looking back forty years later upon that decision, Fran reflected that he was glad he had not spent the last forty years fighting a rear-guard battle and being looked upon as a maverick within the denomination. Because we have just so much time and energy, he believed that if he had stayed he would never have been able to achieve what he had. Because he recognized that the Church is the Body of Christ and not just another organization, he advised, "I personally would not belong to any denomination where there was no hope of recovering the bureaucracy or the seminaries for Jesus Christ."

The Schaeffers made these life-changing decisions prayerfully together, grateful that the Bible gave them truth—objective truth with absolute standards. The Holy Spirit used their Bible study to strengthen and enlighten their moral principles whereby they could, with a sound conscience, take their stand in opposition to their denomination. But Fran also recognized the need in his life for more sweetness, gentleness, love, and kindness. He wanted to express the qualities of love as he stood for truth in the midst of the battle for truth. He battled his temper all his life, but he did develop the kindness that he sought. In all his struggles and decisions, Edith stood with him in prayer and sound counsel. They faced life's challenges together and with their God, knowing that they could trust the promises in His Word.

3

Serving God Together

Francis Schaeffer graduated in early June from Hampden-Sydney College, and Edith and he were married on July 6, 1935. During their first summer together they served as church camp counselors in Michigan and began their early work with children. They learned more about each other and how to deal with their imperfections—especially with Fran's temper that could flare so easily, and Edith's stubbornness once she made a decision. On one occasion she slightly dented their car, and Fran got so angry with her, she vowed (and kept the vow) never to drive a car again. After years of married experience, Edith later taught that marriage is a 90/10 relationship. While there are times where you give 90 percent and the other gives 10 percent, there are also times when your mate gives 90 percent and you only give 10. There are occasions in a marriage where one or the other is just not able to give what is needed. When reflecting upon marriage and illness, Edith learned: "Pain and discomfort need to be shared. One person may be the well one, and one the ill one, but both are involved, which, after all, is what the oneness of marriage—the 'for better and worse, in sickness and in

41

health'—is all about. In spite of being two separate persons, there is a reality of sharing life together which the modern 'scream of rights' or 'scream for independence' knows nothing about!"[1]

Since Edith earned much of Fran's tuition at Westminster Theological Seminary by making clothes for others, she stayed up late at night and sewed in order to share with him the ideas he learned in class. In this way, and also with her own avid reading, Edith acquired the equivalent of a seminary education without the benefit of formal classroom attendance. If you think that Edith must have gotten very little rest, you think right. For most of her life, Edith only needed about three hours of sleep at night. While others slept, she spent the late evening or early morning hours at work, often writing family letters, then *L'Abri Family Letters*, and finally books. They learned the importance of discussing ideas together as a family, and the discussion of ideas became a vital part of their family life as well as in L'Abri with students around the dinner table. When Fran wrote his books, he said that his and Edith's books formed a unit and must be read together.

After Fran's second year at Westminster Theological Seminary in Philadelphia, and following the death of Dr. Machen, the new Presbyterian denomination split. Fran left Westminster and helped found Faith Seminary in Wilmington, Delaware, with Professor MacRae and others. The summer of 1937 found Fran and Edith busily getting the living accommodations ready for staff and students to open Faith Seminary in the fall. Here Fran's background made him a tremendous asset to the endeavor; for example, he salvaged old bathroom fixtures from junkyards to remodel the apartments he was in charge of restoring. He also arranged for his capable father-in-law, Dr. George Seville, to join the faculty and teach missions and introductory Greek. Edith's father continued to teach there for the next seventeen years, until he was eighty. In the midst of all these busy preparations and the founding of a new seminary and denomination, Edith gave birth to Priscilla, their first child, on June 18, 1937.

Because of Fran's hard work and the cooperation of many others, seminary classes began on time in the Faith Bible Presbyterian Church. Fran was the first student to enroll, and he graduated in the first graduating class, maintaining an A average. He was also the first pastor to be ordained in the Bible Presbyterian Church.

Following graduation and ordination, Fran, Edith, and eleven-month-old Priscilla left for Grove City, Pennsylvania. The Covenant Presbyterian Church had called Fran to be their new pastor. The new church consisted of eighteen adults, and on their first Sunday morning few children attended. The parents in their new church believed their children needed to be in a larger Sunday school than the church could provide.

In their first church, Edith began praying without ceasing for her husband while he preached from the pulpit. As the wife of the pastor, she knew this was one of her most important responsibilities. They worked hard together. Using skills he learned from scouting, Fran prepared hot dog roasts in the park to meet new children and eventually win them and their families to Christ and their new church. Edith helped organize and teach in their summer Vacation Bible School. Their first summer, in a church with no Sunday school, seventy-nine children attended the first day of V.B.S., and by the end more than one hundred came.

However, not all of their efforts in Grove City were successful. They tried to reach out to college students at Grove City College, but failed. Little did they realize that they would soon be reaching college students.

From Edith's background in the China Inland Mission and from the inspirational biographies they read, Fran and Edith recognized the importance of prayer. Fran asked a bedridden woman, the wife of an elder in their church, if she would pray for special church needs, hurting people, and his ministry. He went to her house and shared his prayer requests with her, and he always believed that her prayers were an important reason for many wonderful things that happened at Grove City. Fran gave everyone who loved the Lord, no matter what their abilities, an important role in his churches and in L'Abri.

Covenant Presbyterian Church grew so fast under Fran's ministry that in less than three years they built a new building and the membership reached 110. When you consider that Fran had only recently graduated from seminary, this rapid growth seems almost incredible. God blessed their faithfulness, prayer, and hard work, and He called people into the church at a time when believers needed to take a courageous stand for the truth of God's Word. Fran also served as moderator of the Great Lakes Presbytery of the Bible Presbyterian Church, quite an honor and responsibility for such a young man. In the midst of this success, however, with new people coming to church every Sunday, one of Fran's elders suggested that after three years a minister ought to move on to a new church. He felt Fran had probably said all that he had to say! So, Fran and Edith began to pray for God to open another door of service for them.

While in Grove City, on May 28, 1941, Edith gave birth to their second daughter, Susan. A few months later, Fran began serving as the associate pastor of the Bible Presbyterian Church of Chester, Pennsylvania, southwest of Philadelphia. They served there for less than two years. Fran helped them complete a church construction program, but he did not want to be involved in building any more buildings where he thought no more were needed. When he arrived in Chester, they needed Fran's expertise. Because of his education in the trades, his past work with his father, and his experience building a new church in Grove City, he helped with the plans. He climbed up on the scaffolding to work side by side with the members who volunteered their time after work to do much of the actual construction.

The Bible Presbyterian Church in Chester had more than five hundred members, and Fran's background enabled him to talk with shipyard workers and farmers, with professional businessmen and intellectual professors, with young mothers and their children. Fran discovered that people around the world ask essentially the same questions about life and about God, and to properly communicate he needed to learn their language. Learning another's language is a part of what it means to love them. Just as some might learn a foreign dialect to translate the Bible into that language for the first time, so others must learn the language of the farmer, the dockworker, or the philosopher so they can share the Gospel with them in their own language. Fran and Edith learned the language of searching young college students and those the Lord sent them, so they could share the Good News of Jesus Christ with them in terms they would understand. Fran fully supported each person's calling. He never hinted that a doctor might be a more important person than a welder, but he did insist, however, that believers be sure of their calling. The important thing was for them to live as a consistent Christian in whatever vocation they were called.

Because Fran knew that people live in the midst of spiritual battles, he dealt with difficulties and unexpected "moves" in life without being completely shattered by them. He tried not to complain, but looked upon his difficult times and places as opportunities to *give the most to God* and *learn the most from God* in the midst of spiritual warfare. No matter what happened to them, Fran and Edith wanted to maintain integrity, honesty, and truthfulness before God and others. Rather than try to impress people, they wanted to ground their lives in what is real and true. They learned to express their true ideas and feelings, without expressing these in ways that were inappropriate. Over time, God taught them how to express their anger when necessary, and how to control it so they did not damage people or property.

By 1942 Fran's father had become a Christian. He saw the practical application of the Christian faith in Fran's and Edith's lives, something he had not seen before, as Christianity had always appeared irrelevant and Christians had always appeared to be hypocrites. Fran showed him that the ministry can be practical and that many ministers actually do contribute to society instead of being parasites.

The Schaeffers saw the value of people, no matter what their place or position in life. While in Chester, Fran began working with a child with Down syndrome whose parents could not afford the special education she needed. Later, another child with Down syndrome joined them. The parents of the children and many in the church were amazed at what these children accomplished. Children with special needs had a special place in Fran's heart, and this is one of the reasons he worked so hard against abortion and infanticide. One day a very poor family learned that their little girl had an incurable tongue disease, a disease that would very soon take her life. Her parents came to Fran and asked him to anoint their child with oil and pray for her healing. They came to Fran believing the Bible when it declares: "Is any among you afflicted? let him pray. Is any merry? let him sing psalms. Is any sick among you? let him call for the elders of the church; and let them pray over him, anointing him with oil in the name of the Lord: And the prayer of faith shall save the sick, and the Lord shall raise him up; and if he have committed sins, they shall be forgiven him" (James 5:13–15, KJV). Fran prayed for their daughter in obedience to the Scriptures, and the Lord miraculously healed her.

During his long ministry, Fran prayed at other times for people to be healed. Sometimes they were healed and other times they were not. He never claimed to be a faith healer; he only tried to obey the Word of God and leave the results to Him. Just as humility and the primary call to preach and teach prompted Jesus not to place an overemphasis on His healing ministry, so Fran felt called primarily to preach the truth and emphasize practicing God's Word. He quietly demonstrated the truth of Proverbs 11:30, "The fruit of the righteous is a tree of life, and he who wins souls is wise." Fran knew that God had called him to practice evangelism and study to win souls. Later, when Edith wrote *Affliction*, she explained why God answers some prayers for healing but not others.[2] All through their lives Fran and Edith combined prayer with obedient hard work, and God blessed their consistency. They became a clear and open channel for the flow of God's grace into the lives of those around them.

The Schaeffers believed in the specific promises of God given in the Bible, and in faith they acted upon those promises. But they also knew that God sometimes has His own reasons for not answering a prayer for healing or some other request, and that His reason will never contradict His revealed Word or promises. If they were ill, they saw no inconsistency between praying for healing and at the same time taking the best medicine or seeking the best doctors. They believed in using all of God's gifts (the gifts of faith, prayer, physicians, and medicine) in the battle to defeat Satan, sickness, and death. Trouble and sickness are not always a sign of a lack of faith or disobedience. Believers do not need to throw away their medicine to prove their faith in God before He will heal them. The believer's troubles often come from living in a fallen world, from Satan's attacks, and from the sins of others. Perfection will not come until the next world, after Jesus Christ has returned.

4

With Eyes Toward Europe

Before leaving America, the Schaeffer family moved one more time. They did not know where they should go after Fran completed his work in Chester, so they prayed that God would show them where they could honor Him the most. Fran thought God wanted them to go to St. Louis, Missouri, so as Edith sought to know God's definite leading, she prayed for some clear evidence that God wanted them to move to Missouri. Suddenly, in the midst of her prayer for clear leading, the Holy Spirit impressed upon her new words to an old hymn tune. She sang them joyfully and the words expressed her submission to the will of God. This experience convinced her that God had answered her prayer for guidance, and that they should go to the Bible Presbyterian Church in St. Louis.

Fran's father died in 1943, but the Schaeffers rejoiced that he had accepted Jesus Christ as his Lord and Savior. However, Fran's mother continued to hold bitter resentment against God and Fran's work as a minister. In this same year, Fran and Edith began their work in St. Louis. They felt comfortable and loved the people. Fran typically preached two sermons each Sunday and led a Bible study at their Wednesday night prayer meeting. They started a children's Bible class in their basement, and Fran taught the church women how to do the same thing in their homes. Before long, twenty such classes met regularly in the basements of church members throughout the city. Later, Fran and Edith used the lessons they learned from this children's ministry to begin "Children for Christ," a work they would soon take to many churches in Europe. Very slowly, God prepared them to take on greater obligations, and the Schaeffers felt keenly the same sense of responsibility that characterized the apostle Paul: "I am debtor both to the Greeks, and to the Barbarians; both to the wise, and to the unwise" (Romans 1:14, KJV). One of their former church members in St. Louis said of Fran's work there: "He worked hard, and he worked the people hard!"

During their years in St. Louis, Fran continued working beyond his local congregation. On a national level he served in the American Council of Christian Churches. He also began a local council in St. Louis that included the Bible-believing congregations. Fran expressed his social concern and love for all people when he wrote a pamphlet to combat Hitler's antisemitism: "The Bible-believing Christian and the Jew" was distributed by the thousands in the midst of the war years. Later, Edith wrote her popular *Christianity Is Jewish* to break down the barriers between Christians and Jews.[1]

Deborah Ann Schaeffer was born in St. Louis on May 3, 1945. Germany surrendered to the Allies on May 7, so the Schaeffers joined with others in the church and joyfully celebrated Debbie's birth and the war's end. The church began to turn its attention to what it could do to help those ravaged by World War II. They wanted to care for soldiers coming home from the front, and they knew Christians in Europe had suffered terrible losses.

Shortly after Debbie's second birthday, Fran traveled to Europe on behalf of the American Council of Christian Churches and the Independent Board for Presbyterian Foreign Missions (the mission board that J. Gresham Machen had supported so strongly). He went as "The American Secretary, Foreign Relations Department of the American Council of Christian Churches." For three months Fran visited many different churches in order to learn about their situation following the war. He also warned them of the theological dangers their students might face if they studied in some of the American seminaries and Bible colleges, for he knew what false teachings and practices could do to the church.

Fran wrote detailed letters from Europe, and Edith carefully recopied these for publication. He studied the state of the church and the nations, and published his observations. During his ninety days in Europe, Fran met key Christian leaders and spoke at various times before many diverse groups of people. His experience in these European churches increased the reality of his being a part of a greater heritage than he had understood before. He marveled at the various historic sites of the Reformation and the courage of the Reformers. He realized more intensely the call of God for him to carry forward biblical ideas and Reformation principles to his generation. He quickly learned that the state of the church in Europe was far worse than he expected. For example, of sixty pastors in the Geneva State Church, only two or three claimed to be Bible-believing Christians. Some of those he met thought they ought to separate themselves and their churches from the teachings of people like Karl Barth and the ecumenical movement. They did not want to quit preaching the Bible's central teachings about Jesus in order to bring denominations together into one large super church or council. They did not believe that church unity should be more important than upholding the truth of God's Word and doing effective worldwide evangelism.

Fran spoke at meetings and hoped to help develop an International Council of Christian Churches to stand firm for the Bible and the truth of its teachings. He wanted to help create a united front against the theologically liberal takeover of the traditional churches and seminaries. In their life story, *The Tapestry*, Edith made the observation that characterized their thinking: "What a variety of wars there are, and what varied forms of devastation. Inadequate and watered-down food depletes physical bodies, but inadequate, watered-down, and even poisoned spiritual food endangers spiritual life."[2]

While Fran tried to stimulate interest in an International Council of Christian Churches, theological liberals worked to form the World Council of Churches that was formally established in 1948 in Geneva, Switzerland. Since then, the World Council of Churches has challenged Bible-believing churches around the globe and tempted them to compromise their convictions. Fran clearly remembered the words of Dr. Visser't Hooft at the Oslo

Young People's Conference in Norway in July of
1947, one year before Visser't Hooft helped estab-
lish the World Council. Visser't Hooft challenged
the young people to confront the Bible-believing
Christians in their churches in order to "drive the
grayheads out" to have more churches in the World
Council. He also heard the American theologian
Reinhold Niebuhr speak of creating a socialistic interpretation of Christianity. After the event Fran
lamented, "The whole Conference makes me desperately lonely for some Christian contact."[3]

Fran's spiritual depth at the time can be illus-
trated in a letter he wrote to Edith, for he told of his
concern for his people back in St. Louis. "Often in
the midst of other things, one or another person
comes to my mind, and I pray immediately for that
one."[4] Fran's loving concern for people, and the
practical expression of that love in whatever way
possible, even through prayer when apart, always
characterized his ministry and naturally drew people who needed help to his doorstep.

Francis and Edith Schaeffer expressed concern
about false theological doctrines, especially when
these teachings attacked the foundation of faith or
destroyed people's trust in the Word of God. Believing the Bible is true marks the beginning of Christian faith, and Fran discovered in Europe the devastating results when church leaders tried to
destroy people's understanding that the Bible was
truly God's Word. The Schaeffers believed there
should be spiritual experience and emotion in the
believer's life, but experience and emotion should
not be the basis for Christian faith. Christian faith
must be based on the Bible, which is true in all that
it affirms. Christian faith is truth that must be

shared, because it is good news that leads to salvation. Christians live *in* faith and *by* faith, knowing prayer makes a difference. And if joyful experiences are not there sometimes, as in the case of Job in the Old Testament or of Jesus praying in the garden before His arrest and crucifixion, people can still trust in God because they know His Word is true and His promises never fail.[5]

When he went to Europe, Fran had practically no contacts or names of people to see. He went with the continuing prayer that God would take him to the people that he should meet. Edith and the girls prayed along the same lines, and this prayer drew them together while the ocean kept them apart. God answered their prayers and led Fran to people deeply interested in helping form the International Council of Churches. Upon his return to America, Fran received many requests to return and help the embattled theologians, pastors, and churches of Europe.

One of the most unusual experiences of Fran's life took place during his return from Europe. He believed God directly intervened to save his life. The airplane in which he flew over the Atlantic suddenly developed engine trouble and plunged 3,000 feet. A ham radio operator who knew Fran was crossing the Atlantic at that time heard the distress signals and called Edith and the children at home so they could pray. They gathered together as a family and prayed, knowing that Fran's schedule called for him to be on that plane. Fran, of course, prayed too. As they prayed, the engines miraculously started again, and Fran's plane arrived home safely. When he got off the airplane, he heard one of the pilots say that he could not understand how the engines could have started again, that it was absolutely impossible. Fran told them very matter-of-factly, "I know how they started; my heavenly Father started them." The Scriptures teach: "The LORD is far from the wicked: but he heareth the prayer of the righteous" (Proverbs 15:29, KJV).

Fran's trip to Europe was one of his greatest spiritual experiences, but it exhausted him. As he thought of the many problems Christians faced in Europe, he knew there would be a huge battle for truth ahead, but God had used little people to defeat giants before.[6] He thanked God for the unity of the true Church of Christ around the world. He felt it crucial for the true churches to take a stand and separate themselves from the modern forms of unbelief and paganism that characterized liberal theology. Later he wrote:

"Nowhere is practicing the truth more important than in the area of religious cooperation. If I say that Christianity is really eternal truth, and the liberal theologian is wrong—so wrong that he is teaching what is contrary to the Word of God—and then on any basis (including for the sake of evangelism) I am willing publicly to act as though that man's religious position is the same as my own, I have destroyed the practice of truth which my generation can *expect* from me and which it will *demand* of me if I am to have credibility. How will we have *credibility* in a relativistic age if we practice religious cooperation with men who in their books and lectures make very plain that they believe nothing (or practically nothing) of the content set forth in Scripture?"[7]

His report to the Independent Board and the American Council showed many accomplishments.

However, because Fran was burned out, he thought he could never travel again. He did not want to answer the telephone or ever attend another meeting. But during his months of recovery, the Independent Board asked him to be their missionary to Europe. The Schaeffer family struggled to find God's will. Should they leave their happy life in St. Louis? Everyone agreed that the new International Council of Christian Churches needed Fran's help to get it firmly established, but should he leave his work in St. Louis? As he recovered from exhaustion, the Board asked Fran to travel and speak for six months prior to the first meeting of the International Council, which had been scheduled to meet in Amsterdam in August of 1948. To meet these deadlines, the Schaeffers needed to leave for Europe in February, less than six months after his strenuous tour.

What could a small family of five accomplish, sent to the whole continent of Europe so soon after a major war had brought such terrible devastation? How would they survive the lack of almost everything people take for granted? What could they do right in the midst of a massive reconstruction effort? What battles could these two dedicated, Bible-believing Christians win in the struggle for truth against many rich mainline churches forming the World Council of Churches? What could Fran do when rising German theological stars (such as Karl Barth and Paul Tillich) were making such a tremendous impact with their false ideas in seminaries, in churches, and in the world theological scene? How would they inspire people to faith and action, a people who were more exhausted than Fran from fighting a different kind of war? How would they challenge people to keep on battling for the truth, when after the war what they really wanted was peace and unity—almost at any price? "When the foundations are being destroyed, what can the righteous do?" (Psalm 11:3). Perhaps God sent them on ahead to eventually found L'Abri, so they could rescue some of the children and grandchildren of those who followed and taught liberal theology? Did God need them *in Switzerland* to rescue those who had been raised in Bible-believing churches, but who had not been taught how to confront liberal challenges to the Scriptures? What did God want for them at this time in their lives? How would they discover God's will for them?

5

Making Difficult Decisions

The Schaeffers intended to obey God always, but that did not make the decision to go to Europe easy. In 1948, on the last Sunday Francis Schaeffer preached as the pastor of the Bible Presbyterian Church in St. Louis, Edith Schaeffer prayed and wept over his decision to leave the pastorate and become a mission administrator overseas. She envisioned him traveling, speaking, conducting meetings, and writing endless reports. She fervently prayed for the Lord to intervene and keep them in America, because she believed God intended Fran to use his gifts in serving churches and preaching the Bible. As she reasoned with God, she pointed out that Fran loved people and really helped them, so why would God want Fran to be an administrator?

The Lord did not intervene and keep them in their church or find them a new church in America. God's answer to her prayer was a definite "No." They first went to Holland and then to Switzerland with the Independent Board for Presbyterian Foreign Missions. By starting "Children for Christ" classes in churches all across war-torn Europe, they achieved one of their major goals. But if God had answered her prayer the way she wanted, the work of L'Abri would not have begun in 1955, and Dr. Schaeffer would not have developed his influential ideas through his study and discussions with people from all over the world.

God looked at the intention of Edith's heart and did not answer her prayer *to the letter*, but according to her spirit. In her pleading, Edith revealed her strong desire for God to show her husband how and where to serve Him in the best possible ways. The spirit of her prayer indicated that she did not want Fran's good influence diminished, but increased. She wanted him to be more than an administrator, and in answer to prayer he did become far more. Although God did not give her *exactly* what she prayed for by keeping them in America, He did fulfill the intention of her heart or "the spirit of her prayer" by empowering Fran to help people as a pastor in Europe. Later, God enabled him to help Americans in Europe and America.

As they prepared to go to Europe, God expressed His gracious love when Priscilla entered the Philadelphia Children's Hospital. Although her first doctor thought she wasn't really sick, her condition worsened. Then Dr. C. Everett Koop saw her "by accident," and noted that she needed surgery as soon as possible. Hence, as early as 1948, the Schaeffers came to meet Dr. Koop, who had recently become a Christian.[1] While Priscilla had surgery, Fran served as the moderator of the Bible Presbyterian Church Conference which was meeting in Nashville, Tennessee. Fran's thoughtfulness of his daughter at this time made a lasting impression upon Dr. Koop, as he saw the practical expression of the Christian faith that characterized Schaeffer's ministry.

The Schaeffers arrived in Europe when Fran was thirty-six years old, and he spent the next thirty-six years as a missionary. God prepared him for thirty-six years to go to Switzerland, and Fran did not waste those years of preparation. After they arrived in Amsterdam, Schaeffer became the recording secretary for the founding conference of the International Council of Christian Churches. Here, Fran met a young art critic, Hans Rookmaaker. As they talked outside the conference during one of the meetings, Rookmaaker was captivated by Fran's understanding of the Christian faith and its relationship to art. Their conversations at the conference led to a lasting friendship between Hans and Fran. Shortly before Hans died in 1977, he helped Fran create the monumental film series *How Should We Then Live?*

In St. Louis the entire Schaeffer family had spent many Saturdays in art museums learning how to appreciate and evaluate art. Sometimes the children sat and drew the pictures they studied. But with Rookmaaker to stimulate his interest, Fran began seeing the need for more Christian involvement in the arts, and as he toured museums all over Europe, he began to promote more avidly the arts as a valid enterprise for Christian involvement. Fran loved art, and throughout his years in Europe often stopped at a museum to study art and history as he returned home following a Bible study. His friendship with Rookmaaker inspired Fran to write the book *Art and the Bible* for young people who struggled with how to express their artistic aspirations.

After the International Conference, the Schaeffers moved to Lausanne, Switzerland, where Fran began contacting all the people he had met the year before. They began "Children for Christ" in earnest, writing Bible studies for children and sending them all over Europe. The Rookmaakers began teaching and translating the lessons. Other European Christians translated them into their own languages. Theological liberalism so dominated the churches of Europe that children were not taught that the Bible is true. "Children for Christ" materials taught that the Bible is true in the historical areas as well as in the religious and theological areas. Fran and Edith wrote the material for homes and churches in order to provide a Christian alternative to the liberal teachings that were infiltrating the churches.

Fran needed to spend much of his time studying and evaluating a variety of councils of churches and synods all over Europe so he could make recommendations regarding future relationships with them. In the summer of 1949, he attended the Reformed Ecumenical Synod of Amsterdam for two weeks in order to determine their stand on Bible-believing Christianity. With disappointment, he reported to the Bible Presbyterian Church that they should not become a member. He advised that churches and ministers in America should be warned about the synod's rejection of historic, orthodox Christianity.

In Switzerland, the whole family did evangelism as they prayed for the Lord to open doors for them. During their first year in Switzerland, little Priscilla Schaeffer knew French well enough to act as a translator for prospective renters in their boarding house. One evening, Priscilla rushed to tell her family that she had just translated from English into French so a German Jewish woman from Jerusalem could rent a room from Madame Turrian, their landlady. When Fran and Edith met the woman later, she bubbled over with excitement as she spoke about the reestablishment of Israel as a nation. She told about the great expectations of those who believed God might be doing something new in their midst.

In the coming days, God used the perfect timing of these events in Israel to give this woman a receptive mind for what the Schaeffer family had to tell her about Jesus the Messiah. And as the time for her return to Israel approached, the Schaeffers longed to give her a gift, a special Prophecy Edition of the New Testament. However, they did not know where to find one in Switzerland, and they knew they could not send the order to America and get one back in time. So they prayed fervently for a Bible to give, and trusted in God as they went about their daily tasks.

A few days later, on the last afternoon of a conference, Edith heard a man from the Million Testaments Campaigns give a lecture. Afterward, she hurried to the platform and asked him, "Do you have a Prophecy New Testament?" He smiled, reached into his coat pocket, pulled out and gave her exactly what she wanted. What a wonderful, specific answer to their prayers.[2]

After living in their tiny apartment in Lausanne for several months, the Schaeffers learned that their girls needed to go to the mountains for their health, so they rented a chalet in Champéry for the summer. Here, they entertained a host of people going to the Second Plenary Congress of the International Council of Christian Churches. Fran himself spoke at the Congress on "The New Modernism (Neo-orthodoxy) and the Bible." He visited with Karl Barth prior to the meeting to make sure his interpretation of Barth's teaching was accurate, and the speech was later published as an article. Barth taught neo-orthodox theology in an attempt to overcome some of the problems of liberal theology, but he did not believe that the Bible was true in all that it affirms. Neo-orthodoxy is contrary to sound Christian doctrine, which the church had always called "orthodoxy." The name "neo-orthodoxy" sounded contemporary, "new," "relevant," and appealed to many who were misled by its teachings.

After the Schaeffers moved to Champéry, Dr. Otten became their family physician and friend. He was an unbeliever who did not see the value of spiritual concerns as he carried on his busy practice, and did not have time to attend Bible studies or talk much with Fran about Christianity. However, something about the Schaeffer family drew him to them, and his highly intelligent mind began to appreciate Fran's wisdom and approach to faith. The whole family began praying for Dr. Otten and asked God to help them find a way to reach him with the truth. He had already told them that he did not have time to go to Fran's home for Bible Study, and he gave the excuse, "I wouldn't understand it anyway." Finally, the Holy Spirit moved Fran to ask Dr. Otten if he would read some Bible studies that Fran would write personally for him. He could read the studies at his convenience rather than come to his home for Bible studies. Dr. Otten agreed to read the Bible studies, so Edith typed them and Fran delivered them to his office. The Holy Spirit began to move on him as he studied Fran's lessons, but he made no commitment to Christ.

As time passed, their relationship deepened. Dr. Otten saw how the Schaeffer family cared for the villagers and the international students attending the schools around them. He learned that a pastor cared for his parishioners much like a doctor cared for his patients. They not only shared their faith, but they practiced their faith by helping the needy. From some of the villagers, he learned about a Christmas Eve when the Schaeffers had taken a complete American Christmas dinner to an old woman who lived in a small, drafty, broken-down chalet and existed only on bread and cheese. She was amazed to see foods that she had never eaten before and kept asking, "Is this for me? Is this for me?" They explained the meaning of Jesus' birth and told her the meal was a gift from God to her for Christmas. As Dr. Otten learned about their expressions of love in the village, he began to take Fran's lessons more seriously. He treated them more as friends but still chose not to follow Christ.

After more than two years, the truth they shared and the example they set influenced Dr. Otten to come to their home for a serious after-dinner discussion with Fran. Edith needed to leave the room, and later she wrote home, "I knew they had Bibles out and that Fran was progressing toward asking Dr. Otten for a decision. . . . I prayed fervently that this might be the night of salvation for dear Dr. Otten. I had a strange experience, because as the voices were low, I could not know what was being said, and during my fervent and earnest pleading with the Lord, I suddenly was filled with a peace—and even as I attempted to continue my praying—my mind was filled with the phrase, 'It is finished.' I became convinced that the Lord had answered and the need for that particular prayer was finished."[3] Fran later reported that Dr. Otten had given his life to Christ.

The time that Fran and Edith spent praying for Dr. Otten and preparing his lessons drew their hearts closer to him. He could sense their sincere love for him and saw their concern for his salvation. He was not just another number to be won to the Lord, but a real person whose eternal salvation meant much to them. Their prayers enabled him to sense the personal love and concern of Jesus Christ *for him through them.* Much prayer for sinners brings about a bond of unity and love that nothing else will.

The Schaeffers prayed for more than two years for Dr. Otten, and longer for other things. It is tempting to believe that God's answers to prayer are our accomplishments, that the conversion of sinners is our work, and that our faith is the reason for God's answers. When God delays in His answers to prayer, He helps us avoid thinking more highly of ourselves than we ought. When God moved in Dr. Otten's heart and he accepted Christ as Lord, the Schaeffers praised God instead of complimenting themselves.

God had plans for Fran's Bible studies beyond helping Dr. Otten. By helping one person, God enabled Fran to help many. When Fran dictated the studies to Edith, she typed them up with multiple carbon copies. When others wanted the study too, Fran and Edith passed out the carbons to them. When all of the copies were gone, Edith typed them up again with multiple carbons, and these too were given away. Finally, Edith typed stencils and they used a mimeograph machine to make multiple copies of the book. When the stencils wore out, she typed more stencils. In 1972, *Basic Bible Studies* was published as a real book. What Fran and Edith were willing to do and did do for one person resulted in many people learning the Bible's teaching and accepting Christ as their Savior. For more than twenty years *Basic Bible Studies* has been used by groups meeting in homes and churches to introduce non-Christians and new Christians to the Bible.[4]

American military personnel have been stationed in Europe since the close of World War II, and servicemen visited the Schaeffers as soon as Fran and Edith moved out of the city and into a Swiss chalet. Visits by the servicemen convinced them of how much God wanted to do in their lives in answer to prayer. God prepared them well in advance for each new step that He intended for them to take. One Sunday afternoon a young American soldier visited the Schaeffers, and their conversation turned to a pastor in Zurich that the young man knew. Neither Fran nor Edith had met this pastor, who had a young family like their own. He had been voted out of his church for emphasizing God's grace and some other essential biblical "orthodox" doctrines. At first, the pastor tried some secular jobs to support his family; then, God led him into teaching the Bible in homes, traveling to other countries to preach, and in supporting his family by faith through prayer. As they discussed this pastor and his problems, they heard a knock at the door. After opening the door, they saw the very pastor they were talking about. The pastor spoke

only German and the American soldier interpreted
so the Schaeffers could understand.

God orchestrated this encounter to help the pastor from Zurich who needed to know that there were
many others (especially Americans) who still believed as he did. And God wanted to impress upon
the Schaeffers how He could provide for a pastor
and his family if they took a stand for God and truth
in spite of the cost. God's teaching the Schaeffers
about courage, obedience, and prayer through this
man made such an impression upon Edith that
when she wrote home she asked people to pray for
him. They did not take these prayers for granted,
but praised God that those who lived far away could
enter into their work with them through prayer.
They believed prayer was real work, just as many
other types of Christian work and physical labor
take great effort.

The Schaeffers' contacts with American servicemen opened new doors for them. In 1950, about four
years after the liberation of the prisoners from the
Nazi death camp of Dachau, Fran and Edith went
to that city to teach a two-week Vacation Bible
School for the American children of the soldiers stationed there. They wept when they saw the actual
gas chambers and torture cells run by the German
medical doctors before everything was cleaned up
and Dachau was made into a museum. Man's in-
humanity to man was graphic, as some people still
lived in a displaced persons camp. The Schaeffers
returned there again for the filming of *Whatever
Happened to the Human Race?* when they compared
the holocaust to abortion, infanticide, and "mercy
killing" now going on with government sanctions in
many countries around the world. The low view of

human life in Germany during Hitler's rise to power prepared the way for the atrocities of his government. Schaeffer knew that the low view of human life in America and around the world would lead to even greater atrocities, especially with the new medical technologies that can be used for either good or evil. Schaeffer taught, and he has been proven right, that legalized abortion would lead to an epidemic of child abuse and murder by parents who did not understand the value of all human life as created in the image of God.

The Schaeffers continued to help military personnel in Europe seeking to know Christ and what it means to obey Him in the totality of life. But even during the war, when Fran was a pastor in America, he talked to the men going overseas and reminded them of the ungodly attitude they could develop when placed in situations where they would need to take the lives of their fellowman. They must not hate their enemies, but must realize the need to defend freedom and truth in a fallen world. Fran continued to remind those who fought on the side of right not to aim at "getting rid of the negative at any cost—rather praying that the negatives might be faced in the proper attitude."[5]

6

Troubles Bring New Opportunities

By 1950, Francis and Edith Schaeffer became concerned about problems within "The Separated Movement," a movement that encouraged the Bible-believing Christians to separate themselves from liberal congregations and denominations. Fran began to warn of the danger of getting discouraged with the battle and then compromising with the enemy or withdrawing from the conflict. He also warned against becoming cold and hard of heart as one served the Lord. He saw some people fighting for orthodox belief, and then becoming unorthodox in practice when they lost a Christlike spirit and love for others. He challenged them to remember that the Lord's work requires self-denial, self-sacrifice, and hard work. He strongly emphasized the need for Bible-believing Christians to produce both scholarly material and warm devotional material. He saw the real danger of Bible-believing people, involved in the battle for truth, losing the love God commands us to demonstrate daily to everyone. In *The Tapestry*, Edith quoted from an article Fran wrote at this time, "There is a danger of developing in our age of necessary contending, a will to win, rather than a will to be right. . . . Our daily prayer should be that our loving Lord will keep His arms so about us that we will neither waver in the fight nor allow the Devil to destroy us from within."[1] "To be right" includes loving others as we share the truth with them, so we can lead them to embrace the God of love. "A will to win" can quickly lead to saying hurtful, unloving things that can destroy those God loves and drive them away from God.

In one of his later books, *True Spirituality*, Schaeffer also warned against pride when you know you are right and the other person is wrong:

> In the midst of being right, if self is exalted, my fellowship with God can be destroyed. It is not wrong to be right, nor to say that wrong is wrong, but it is wrong to have the wrong attitude in being right, and to forget that my relationship with my fellow men must always be personal and as equals. If I really love a man as I love myself, I will long to see him be what he could be on the basis of Christ's work, for that is what I want or what I should want for myself on the basis of Christ's work.[2]

The year 1951 marked the beginning of a spiritual revival and renewal of Francis Schaeffer's life and ministry. He had been in Europe for three years. He faced the crisis of how best to communicate the gospel in a culture that was foreign to him. He struggled to give people, recently devastated mentally, physically, and spiritually by two World Wars, exactly what they needed in the area of truth and practical concern. Not only was the culture foreign to him, but much of the so-called Christianity in the churches of Europe was not biblical.

At the same time, he was concerned about the lack of love that was so apparent in many of the orthodox Christian churches he knew in "The Separated Movement." Too many people had developed a hard, inflexible attitude in their standing for the truth. Too much of true Bible-believing Christianity had become unloving and hateful in practice. He was disturbed about the reality of Christianity, if the result of believing was becoming unloving. Some enjoyed debating and winning battles more than winning someone to Christ by expressing a loving faith. The fact that Fran himself grew in this regard can be shown by his comments right before he died: when someone asked if he thought he would win his battles for truth, he replied, "I don't know, but at least I have fought for what is right. It is not whether we can win or lose, but whether or not we are faithful, loyal, and true to the Lord Jesus Christ." This remained Fran's goal in his final book, *The Great Evangelical Disaster*. It warned evangelical churches about the temptation to fall away from belief in the Scriptures, even as many churches had done fifty years earlier.

Fran came to many of his ideas on true spirituality, of the need to speak the truth with love, after a transforming spiritual experience occurred soon after they moved to Chalet Bijou in Champéry. He needed to be alone with his thoughts, so when the weather was good he hiked in the mountains. When the weather was bad, he walked and thought in the chalet hayloft. He read his Bible and prayed. He told Edith that he was taking his faith all the way back to his early days of agnosticism (of not knowing whether God was really there or not) to see if Christianity was really true. He wanted to re-think everything and see if there were good and sufficient reasons to be a Christian. He frightened Edith because of his intense and serious commitment to throw his faith away if he could not find its reality. She prayed earnestly for him as he insisted on walking this road alone. While walking in the hayloft one day, the Holy Spirit poured His power into Fran in a mighty way. Fran renewed his Christian commitment, and this became the turning point in his life. What he learned from that time he later incorporated into his books *The Church Before the Watching World* and *True Spirituality*.[3]

Fran's "hayloft experience" gave him the firm conviction that God is truly, objectively *there* as the Bible describes Him, whether people think God is there or not. God convinced him that the Bible is true in all that it teaches and that it applies to the whole of life. Fran learned again by experience that the spiritual reality of love and holiness, which is given by the Holy Spirit, must be present in our lives, especially so while fighting for the truth.

During his walk he not only came to some intellectual decisions, but he had the deep spiritual experiences of other great men of God before being called to a greater and more influential work. He found himself walking and praising God. He began to "feel" songs of praise well up from within himself. He began to sing and write poetry again. He learned what the finished work of Christ meant in his present experience; therefore, he began to emphasize more that people should become Christians based upon the objective truths of Christian teaching—truths that could be thought through and analyzed again and again based upon new knowledge. Truths that could bear the weight of thorough investigation. He stressed that a personal, subjective relationship with the Lord Jesus Christ flows from our accepting His finished work upon the Cross in our behalf.

In 1951, Fran recaptured in his life what many of the Reformers taught on the devotional level. Fran's hayloft experience did not lead him to think that faith is grounded in experience. Christian faith is grounded in the objective revelation of the God of the Bible, but experiencing a relationship with God that continues throughout life should follow a person's new birth. He recognized that his own lack of the reality of the presence of God in his life was related to his ignorance about the meaning of the finished work of Christ in his present life, and time spent in the hayloft helped him overcome that ignorance. He began to obey Christ in everything from a real heartfelt love for Him. Obedience to Christ ceased to be a burden upon his back, and became the joy of his life. He interpreted his experience, lectured about it, and then wrote about the work of the Holy Spirit in *True Spirituality*.

After his hayloft experience, a new door opened to him, a door that led him to acting more upon his knowledge of the Christian faith. He came to realize the necessity of being more open to Christ in prayer, so that Jesus Christ could bear His fruit in his life. He learned that if he was to become a more effective agent of God, he must allow Christ to work more within him. He believed Christians must know the power of the resurrected Christ in their own lives in the present, so he began to insist that the Christian life involves a daily reliance upon the

Holy Spirit within us as a constant act of faith. He taught that Christians need to think and act upon the promises of Scripture, as well as His commands. They need to ask God to fulfill His promises and bear fruit in their lives for the sake of a world needing to know Him. By faith, the Christian should know an ever-increasing, moment-by-moment experiential relationship with Christ and the whole Trinity. This wonderful spiritual experience of Fran's marked the real beginning of L'Abri. It shows the truly experiential side of his faith. Because the hayloft experience was so deeply personal, it cannot be adequately described; however, Fran's experience occurred after he increased his knowledge and understanding of biblical faith and practice. Then he committed himself to seeking the daily empowering of the Holy Spirit so he could serve God more effectively and bless others.

Fran never again questioned his loving relationship with God. Even in his last years he often woke in the morning and sang Christian songs of praise to his God without being self-conscious. Sometimes the people downstairs in his home would hear him talking to somebody, but they knew that no one else was upstairs with him. They would listen carefully and hear that he was pausing from his work to pray to his God, his heavenly Father. He was never ashamed of being a Christian or knowing God. One summer day, as he walked along the beach among the sunbathers, he mentioned to those with him, "All these people are worshiping the wrong 'sun [son].' " Then he began to sing softly for all to hear, "Jesus loves me, this I know, for the Bible tells me so."

Following his revival experience, Fran asked

Edith a question he began to ask others over and over again: "Edith, I wonder what would happen to most churches and Christian work if we awakened tomorrow, and everything concerning the work of the Holy Spirit, and everything concerning prayer, were removed from the Bible. I don't mean just ignored, but actually cut out—disappeared. I wonder how much difference it would make?"[4] He wondered how much Christian work would just continue in its dead sameness, devoid of spiritual power and reality, because those in the work were unaware of the power of the Holy Spirit and the power of prayer. How many Christians had ceased to rely upon the work of God in their lives, and so were doing their work in their own strength? When Fran asked some of the leaders in his denomination questions like these, it soon got him in trouble.

In Switzerland, Fran was more than an administrator. Edith had prayed that Fran would be able to continue preaching in a church. In answer to those prayers, before their first Christmas in Champéry, a French-speaking minister asked Pastor Schaeffer to provide a Christmas Eve service in English for the Protestant Church in Champéry. Prior to World War I, an English lady had built a chapel for Protestant worship (especially for the English-speaking tourists) in this Roman Catholic canton.* She had built it near the train station for everyone to see, and had included Scripture texts on the inside walls as a silent testimony to the Gospel. On Christmas Sunday, Fran preached to about 150 worshipers, including girls from England and boys from Scotland. Following the service, he

---

* A "canton" is a state within the nation of Switzerland.

learned that he could conduct weekly services in the church for as long as they lived in Champéry. What an answer to Edith's prayers! Within two years from the time they left America, Francis Schaeffer was preaching "in a real church" again, and he continued to conduct Christmas Eve services in that church for the next thirty-two years. Years before they needed a home in the Alps and a church in which to preach, the Lord had provided for their needs.

Francis August Schaeffer V, "Franky," was born August 3, 1952. Two months before his birth, Fran and Edith ministered in Spain and Portugal. Here they witnessed the persecution of Christians by the state, inspired by the Roman Catholic Church. They grieved when they discovered that the poor Protestant Christians had already come under the influence of teaching similar to Karl Barth's. The truth of the Bible was worth being persecuted for, but the teaching that the Bible was full of error would only destroy these people in the present and in the future.

In 1953 the Schaeffers began their missionary furlough by returning to America. They needed a vacation from missionary work, but all missionary furloughs become a different type of work. On furloughs, missionaries travel to supporting churches to talk about their work and encourage support for it. This would hardly be a vacation in any sense of the word, just a change of location. Fran taught pastoral theology at Faith Theological Seminary for the year, and fulfilled a series of speaking engagements around the country to inform the churches about their work.

Before they left for America, they had no idea

where they would live, so they prayed intensively. In the middle of Fran's asking God to show them a place to live, as he was walking on their balcony in Switzerland, he heard a voice answer him. The voice was so clear that it was as if another person walking with him had spoken three simple words, "Uncle Harrison's house." He wrote to his uncle immediately and received an amazing affirmative answer. His only other experience of hearing a voice during prayer was in response to a prayer asking God to forgive him.

Reflecting upon his hayloft experience, Fran wrote a series of talks he gave many times during his furlough. He called these simply: "Sanctification I, II, III, IV, V." They stirred a controversy, as Fran pleaded for speaking the truth in love as we stand for the holiness of God. Also, he emphasized the necessity for Christians to rely upon the power of God to minister through them, and not to rely only upon their own strength. At various times in his meetings, Fran encountered misunderstandings of his ideas. Rumblings began about whether or not he should be sent back to Switzerland. After he gave the seminary graduation speech, a person approached Edith and sternly warned that the denomination was going to split! Some of the denomination's leadership thought Fran was making a power play. Edith explained the controversy this way: Fran's message at graduation "had been so contrary to what was normally given of the centrality of pointing out the errors of *others*. Objections came to such statements as: 'There is no source of power for God's people—for preaching or teaching or anything else—except Christ himself. Apart from Christ, anything that seems to be spiritual power is actually the power of the flesh.' "[5]

Highland College awarded Fran the honorary Doctor of Divinity degree in May 1954. By the time of the synod meeting in Greenville, North Carolina, disagreement with Dr. Schaeffer and his position became clear. With the five talks he gave on sanctification (later expanded into the book *True Spirituality*) he insisted, in a way that many were not yet ready to hear, that the church and denomination needed both reformation and revival. He said there must be a return to the sound teaching of the Bible (reformation) and a practice of that teaching under the power of the Holy Spirit (revival). The Schaeffers didn't know whether they could return to the mission field or not. Battle lines were drawn, but not just over the Schaeffers. The denomination did split a year later (1955). The year 1955 also marked the founding of Covenant College, Covenant Seminary, The Evangelical Presbyterian Church, and the Schaeffers' L'Abri Fellowship in Switzerland.

The conflict within the denomination became so heated that in the middle of their seventeen-month furlough the Lord showed the Schaeffers that they would need to pray for the funds to return to Switzerland. They decided not to write letters describing their plight and requesting money, but to take their need to the Lord alone in prayer. The girls made a thermometer, and colored it in as they received funds for their boat fare. They needed their ticket money by July 29, 1954, to make reservations, but it came in so slowly they had to remind the girls that God might be showing them that His will was for them to remain in America rather than return to Switzerland, and all they wanted was

God's will for their lives. From unexpected sources, God met their needs right before the deadline, and the Schaeffers sent for their tickets home.

Through their prayers for boat passage, God reminded the Schaeffers that He would often providentially use money, its lack or provision, to show them His will. By His Spirit and through circumstances, He gave them enough warning to begin praying soon enough for Him to work and give them the answer in a way that would do them the most good spiritually. Rather than wait until the last minute, they began praying for money in the middle of their furlough. God could have answered their last-minute prayers and sometimes did; however, this time God inspired them to begin praying immediately and continue praying for almost eight months. God often prefers to show us the need for persistent prayer to build up our relationship with Him and increase our faith when He gives the answer. Through much prayer, God and His will often become more important than the answer we want, and God wants us to be in that state of heart. After eight months of prayer and patient waiting, the money for their boat passage came the day it was needed. What a wonderful way for God to inspire real rejoicing for His answers to prayer! And what a tremendous preparation for the beginning of L'Abri!

The Schaeffers returned to their mission field in Switzerland, but without the express blessing of their mission board. Some people were angry with them, because they thought Dr. Schaeffer was trying to take over the leadership of the denomination. Rather than try to take over the leadership of a denomination or found a new church, however, Fran and Edith chose to bury themselves in a tiny village in Switzerland. They continued to seek and to do the Lord's work prayerfully and in the Lord's way, to see what fruit He might bring forth from the tiny grains of wheat of this one family. Toward the end of his life, Dr. Schaeffer marveled at how much God had accomplished that never could have been done if he had stayed in America to fight battles within the denomination.

After the Schaeffers returned to Switzerland, their mission board acted upon Fran's emphasis for "the need of cleansing on the part of Christians, and of being dependent upon the Lord's strength and in the power of the Holy Spirit, and of standing for truth with love."[6] However, they acted the very opposite from what Fran advised. The Schaeffers received a letter from the board, announcing that their salary would be cut by $100 per month. Furthermore, letters began to be sent to their supporting churches, expressing opposition to Schaeffer's teaching and work. Even Christian groups in other countries, with whom the Schaeffers had worked closely for several years, received letters warning them of the Schaeffers' influence.

How could they survive and what would they do in a foreign country far from home, with virtually no funds to stay and no funds to leave, with their material supply lines being severed in salary cuts, and with dire warnings about them being sent to those who knew and cared for them?

7

Living by Faith Alone

When Francis and Edith Schaeffer began L'Abri and chose to live on the basis of faith instead of a regular salary, they did not take a leap in the dark. For much of their ministry, and especially in the early years of the 1950s, they had been learning to walk in faith and truth one step at a time. They had prayed for a place to live while on furlough, and God had given them an immediate answer. They had prayed for money to return to Switzerland, and God had provided the money in answer to prayer. A whole series of God's specific answers to prayer preceded their beginning of L'Abri. They remembered how God had met the needs of Hudson Taylor and other missionaries when they prayed. When the Scriptures also encouraged them in this ministry, they began L'Abri with good and sufficient reasons to think that this was God's will for their lives, and that He would be faithful in meeting all of their real needs for ministry. No leap in the dark was involved, but there was certainly a very exciting step of faith in totally relying upon God.

Ordinarily, when we think of living by faith, we think of missionaries, evangelists, pastors, and revivalists who trust solely in God for their food, clothing, shelter, and other needs, rather than relying on a church or missionary society to give them a regular salary. When the Schaeffers founded L'Abri, God called them to a new way of living by faith alone *for them*. However, before God called them to take this step of faith, He providentially taught them some lessons about prayer and gave them the courage to rely on Him alone and upon those God moved in answer to prayer to provide for them without their asking people for money.

In January of 1955, Edith was reading from Isaiah as a part of her daily reading and time of prayer. When she came to Isaiah 2:2–3, she read: "It shall come to pass in the latter days that the mountain of the house of the LORD shall be established as the highest of the mountains, and shall be raised above the hills; and all the nations shall flow to it, and many peoples shall come, and say: 'Come, let us go up to the mountain of the LORD, to the house of the God of Jacob; that he may teach us his ways and that we may walk in his paths'" (RSV). She believed God was speaking directly to her through Isaiah, that it was His promise for a L'Abri in the mountains of Switzerland.

The promise from God's Word, given in the context of Edith's praying about L'Abri, sustained her and Dr. Schaeffer in the trying difficulties ahead. This type of answer to prayer while reading through the Scriptures guided Edith's work throughout the years. Real answers to prayer gave them courage to keep on following God in the midst of very real trials. For example, Edith explains about prayer in *The Tapestry*:

Prayer is a moment-by-moment example of the

reality of the validity of choice. God himself has given us this communication for a diversity of reasons. One is that our calling upon the Father in Jesus' name, and in the power of the Holy Spirit, is time after time a slap in Satan's face, that proves the victory of Christ's death to defeat the primary purpose of Satan's temptation and the resultant separation of Adam and Eve, human beings, people, from communication with God.[1]

After his furlough there were many misunderstandings and personality clashes over Dr. Schaeffer and his public stands. Letters flew back and forth across the Atlantic as Dr. Schaeffer tried to clarify his positions on sanctification, faith, the work of the Holy Spirit, and man's freedom and responsibility. Later some called him a humanist or a rationalist, because he tried to "think with" people and appeal to their reason to convince them to accept with the empty hands of faith the finished work of Jesus Christ on the Cross. From battles such as these within the church and without, he wisely decided that talking about people and organizations (rather than about ideas) would not be helpful. In their discussions at L'Abri, and in their many group discussions over the years, Dr. Schaeffer and Edith insisted that organizations and personalities should not be discussed. To them, discussing ideas and thinking about the consequences of ideas would have a better and longer-lasting effect for decision-making than criticizing institutions or individuals.

The battle is really for truth against falsehood, and the people who came to L'Abri needed to learn how to analyze the ideas that organizations or people expressed. At L'Abri, the Schaeffers did not just pigeonhole people into categories and escape responsibility for thinking about ideas. They did not want people to leave L'Abri saying, "The Schaeffers think this person or that group is wrong." Understanding how ideas influence the choices you make and the lifestyle you choose is of more lasting value as you analyze the world you encounter than judging individual personalities. Organizations and personalities change; they come and go. You become what you think about, and what you do relates to the way you think. Dr. Schaeffer did not offer easy outs to people who did not want to think. He believed that one of the most lasting effects of discussion and study should be the knowledge of how to think clearly and logically, and of how to discern right ideas from wrong ways of thinking.

Consequently, no ideas were off limits for discussions at L'Abri. Just as Dr. Schaeffer and his family were to help others from their understanding of God and reality as based upon the Bible, so they learned from the many people who came. Many came to discuss books of all types. They wanted to talk about music, the arts, philosophy, theology, science, ethics, politics, law, drug use, current events around the world, medicine, alternative lifestyles, and the different religions. All these discussions led some people to see how Christianity relates to the whole of life, to all disciplines and endeavors. Many of these discussions took place around the dinner table, as Edith made sure every person enjoyed a family atmosphere at L'Abri. Many who came to L'Abri had never known a real family. Other discussions took place as everyone pitched in to work in the garden or prepare dinner or clean the house and grounds. Some students learned to work with their hands for the first time, and every student worked four hours each day in addition to their studies. Those who took part in L'Abri learned practical life skills, the value of work, and the importance of balance in one's life.

The first four members of L'Abri, making up the official board, were George H. Seville, George Exhenry (who had been converted in Champéry and was willing to take the persecution that came from his publicly being a Christian), and Francis and Edith Schaeffer. The children became a vital part, as the whole family made the decision together to begin L'Abri, and as they all shared in its work.

It would be impossible to say everything that could be said about L'Abri. However, there are certain key events and dates that should be briefly summarized. These will help you see that God had led the Schaeffers for several years to begin this work. They did not do so out of a sense of desperation, even though their mission board had placed them in a desperate situation. They founded L'Abri so they could keep on teaching the truth.

They took a step of faith based upon God's work in their lives up to that point. As early as 1949 the Schaeffers had been talking to students of many different backgrounds about Christianity. Zoroastrians, Buddhists, Hindus, atheists, agnostics, liberal Christians, Roman Catholics, and others of various anti-Christian and Christian views had been coming to their door. These students were from all over the world: Haiti, India, Argentina, Canada, England, Scotland, America, and the Scandinavian countries. The Schaeffers had been in a ministry with students for more than six years prior to L'Abri's founding and their decision to minister to students on the basis of trusting in the Lord for His provision. This is to emphasize again that in their work they did not take "leaps in the dark" any more than Dr. Schaeffer taught that Christian faith was a "leap in the dark" or a "leap of faith." Many similar enterprises have failed on this very account: people have leaped into a work without any clear knowledge that the work is truly God's will for them. Or, they have started a new work without waiting for God to make the necessary preparations in advance. If L'Abri had jumped into something without any idea about where it might lead, or without knowing that God had led them to make that decision, it would have hindered their witness to the fact that people become Christians for good and sufficient reasons; they do not take a blind leap of faith. The aim of L'Abri, from its founding to the present, has been to walk prayerfully after good and sufficient reasons have been given by God for the next step.

From the time of Edith's answer to prayer about L'Abri, up to and even beyond its official founding in June of 1955, times were not easy. Satan attacked and buffeted them all along the way, but what Satan meant for evil God meant for good, and worked to their benefit. Had it not been for her promise from God in the context of the prophet Isaiah, Edith could have felt that the trying events were designed by God to move them *from* Switzerland. Instead, she saw them as part of the spiritual warfare in which they were deeply involved. By this time, the Lord had transformed her stubborn streak into the character traits of perseverance and persistance. These traits led her to push on through trials till L'Abri found a home in the Alps.

On February 14, 1955, Swiss officials notified Fran and Edith that they must leave Switzerland because they had made a "religious influence" in Champéry. Someone had complained that the Schaeffers had led some of the villagers to turn away from Roman Catholicism. Officials forbid the Schaeffers to return to Champéry for two years. At the very time things began to break apart in their mission work (with the denomination seeking to make things difficult for them), the Schaeffers lost their home in Switzerland by an uncharacteristic government edict. If they wanted to stay in Switzerland, they needed to find some other home in some other canton.

They searched diligently for a new place to live, but they could not afford any house they were shown. Finally, in the midst of a snowstorm, Edith found Chalet les Mélèzes* in Huémoz in the canton of Vaud. Previous owners named Mélèzes after the beautiful *mélèzes* or larch trees that grew between the chalet and the road. The day she saw Mélèzes, Edith prayed for a sign from the Lord, that if He wanted them to buy the house He would send them $1,000 *the very next day* in the mail. She had never been so bold and asked for something that seemed impossible before, because someone would have needed to put the check in the mail *before* she prayed! But she prayed and believed that with God all things are possible, and God could answer a prayer "backwards."[2] That is, God can answer prayer even before we pray by influencing people to act and us to pray with perfect timing. The next

---

* Pronounced "ma-lez."

day, before she left with Fran on the train to show him the chalet, they received their mail—and found a check for $1,000. Some dear friends in Ohio had written in their letter that "the Lord, they felt, had led them to send it to the Schaeffers to start a fund to buy a house where young people would come to learn more about the Lord Jesus."[3] The Holy Spirit had provided His answer through friends even before He had inspired her to go boldly to the Lord with an "impossible" request. This three-story chalet, completely furnished, would cost them about $17,000, but they had to trust in the Lord's leading for the rest of the money to be given *in time* to make the necessary payments. When the first payment was due, they counted their gifts in their "house" fund, and discovered that they had $3.52 more than they needed. For most of the time in L'Abri, and even to this day, God works just this closely to provide their needs—one day at a time.

To provide for those He sent, God had to give the Schaeffers more than a $1,000 earnest payment for their home. To stay in Huémoz, they had to make a $7,366 down payment on Chalet les Mélèzes by May 31, 1955. And they had only sixty days to pray for that amount. By May 22, they had received only $4,915.69, so they continued to persevere in prayer. Only on the last day did they receive the rest of what they needed. In answer to prayer alone (and without soliciting funds), God had motivated 156 people to send them money. God's evident display of faithfulness encouraged them to move ahead, and Fran resigned from his mission board on June 5 to *officially* begin L'Abri. These remarkable answers to prayer regarding their home in the mountains for L'Abri gave the Schaeffers the courage to write their mission board and resign. God had enabled them to move to Huémoz by April 1, the deadline set by the government. God had provided the money for them to purchase their home by May 31, the deadline set by the chalet's owners.

In addition to providing money, God provided people for the Schaeffers to serve. Even before Fran resigned, God began L'Abri by sending people in answer to prayer. On the weekend of May 6, 1955, Priscilla brought home from college a girl who had many questions. From that day forth, God began leading a stream of young people with questions to their door. L'Abri came to be a spiritual "shelter" for people with real and honest questions. God's hand was so obviously in the work that when Dr. Schaeffer courageously resigned from his mission board, he asked that all salary be cut off immediately. He told them that God had led them to begin L'Abri Fellowship. The Schaeffers had had the reality of the existence of God demonstrated to them in real ways up to that point, and they began L'Abri simply from a desire "to show forth by demonstration, in our life and work, the existence of God."[4]

They made plans to achieve this goal in specific ways: they would pray in four different areas. First, rather than appeal to others to send them money, they would pray for God to meet their material needs. Second, they would pray for God to send the people He wanted to L'Abri, and keep all others away. Third, they would pray for God's leading every day, rather than planning the work themselves. Fourth, they would pray for God to send the people He wanted to join them in the work.

As L'Abri grew, the Schaeffers knew they needed a study center. With so many coming from different nations, they needed taped lectures and recorders, books, and a quiet place for people to listen, read, and think. Once again, they turned to God and asked Him to provide all these things to help others. After Edith's cousin Marion, who had served as a missionary to Egypt, left $20,000 to L'Abri in her will, they completed the Farel House study center and bought the first tape recorders for the Schaeffers' teaching tapes. They named Farel House after William Farel, the Swiss Reformer who convinced Calvin to stay in Geneva and make it into a model Christian community. Four hundred years before the beginning of L'Abri, Farel had preached near Huémoz. He was one of the warmest and most understanding of the Reformers. They wanted Farel, with his Christian spirit and temper, to be a model for every student at L'Abri. Fran taped lectures for Farel House students, and L'Abri still makes these tapes available by mail. Many Egyptian young people meet and study at Farel House, so cousin Marion's missionary work to Egypt continues. Francis and Edith's missionary work showed that in addition to missionaries going to a foreign country to reach the native people, God can also send people from around the world to a missionary's door or study center.

In their lectures and way of life, the Schaeffers did not put the Christian faith into a compartment or "box" unrelated to life and separated from different aspects of living. They called both new and old Christians to walk in truth at all times and in all places. They taught believers to confront wrong ideas and actions with love for others and out of respect for a holy God. They encouraged people to learn about the Christian faith and to be open to learning about different views so they could help others become Christians. At different times in history, Satan tempted people to believe different and wrong systems of thought. Dr. Schaeffer warned: "A world spirit has always existed from the fall of Satan and of Adam and Eve. The creature wants to be autonomous from the Creator. This world spirit takes on different forms in each decade. We can be infiltrated by that form of the world spirit that surrounds us."[5] He wanted to teach people how to recognize the form the world spirit was taking in their decade, so they could resist and help others resist its infiltration.

Fran and Edith had met at church in the midst of a theological battle, and theological battles accompanied them throughout life. Until parted by death, they stood side by side for the same truths. To understand their ministry and mission work, two major problems they faced must be comprehended. During their years in seminary and following, these two problems plagued the Schaeffers as they sought greater reality in their Christian faith and strived to draw closer to God. The first problem became a keynote of Dr. Schaeffer's teaching and private conversations; that is, *Christians must always stand for holiness and love at the same time.* After study and prayer, he came to believe that this can never be done in a person's own strength. It can only be done through the power and presence of the Holy Spirit in the Christian's life. God gave the Holy Spirit so He could help Christians live Christlike. Fran's battles with his own imperfections drove him closer and closer to Christ and the indwelling Holy Spirit. When he talked to others who disagreed with him, he faced the difficulty of making "a simultaneous exhibition of the holiness of God and the love of God." In his early ministry, he stood for God's holiness and for orthodoxy; but sometimes he did not display the love of Christ for others as he spoke. This serious problem marred his relationship with some. After Fran's hayloft experience, he challenged people to stand for God's holiness and truth, and at the same time show the love of Christ for others. By this time, in his battle for truth, God had transformed Fran's flaring anger into something better than "righteous indignation." He had learned to follow the Bible's teaching: "Put on the new self, which in *the likeness of* God has been created in rightousness and holiness of the truth. Therefore, laying aside falsehood, SPEAK TRUTH, EACH ONE *of you*, WITH HIS NEIGHBOR, for we are members of one another. BE ANGRY, AND *yet* DO NOT SIN; do not let the sun go down on your anger, and do not give the devil an opportunity" (Ephesians 4:24–27, NASB).

The second problem that disturbed them was the notion that every action or decision people make is in some way caused or predetermined by God. If this is the case, choice is not real choice. Pushed to extremes, this view says that prayer makes no difference, because in some mysterious way God has already determined what He is going to do or not do, anyway. With this concept, people cannot pray to God and expect their requests will make any real difference in history. People can only make prayers of thanksgiving or confession. The Schaeffers believed that people make real choices, and these choices make a real difference in history. You write your own autobiography by the choices you make and the things you do; even as God works, makes choices, and does things in history that affect your life. People are accountable for their choices. God holds people responsible for what they say and do. Because people are responsible and accountable for their actions, sin is real and they are guilty of committing sins against a holy God. Because they are truly guilty, they need Jesus Christ as their Savior. Human life is not "just a piece of theater" with God pulling all the strings, or with people living out a script written by God before they were born. By trying to understand and explain how people's choices are real and make a significant difference, the Schaeffers helped many confused people.

Fran and Edith dealt with many problems presented by these two perspectives. How can believers show God's love and holiness in their lives when they fight for truth? How can believers uphold the sovereign glory of God and at the same time hold themselves and others accountable for their decisions and behavior? In very practical ways, by their lives and prayers, the Schaeffers sought to demonstrate the presence of God and the truth of God to their generation. Because they decided to stand for God and His way as revealed in the Bible, they often paid a price for these decisions when others got angry with them.

From time to time, Fran and Edith became involved in theological controversy. As their faith matured, they learned how to disagree with someone else and at the same time show that person that they actually cared for them. One theological professor, who for years often publicly criticized the Schaeffers' way of helping people become Christians, retired and then wrote a long, critical treatment of Fran's view of the Christian faith and evangelism. Dr. Schaeffer responded privately to some in L'Abri and said, "I would hate to think that I might spend my retirement doing something like that!" Still, he kept all of this professor's works available for study at L'Abri, while withdrawing his own tapes that discussed this person's views and their disagreements. Dr. Schaeffer learned that a public response to his critics seldom helped, and he simply did not have the time—he preferred to discuss ideas rather than personalities or personal differences.[6] After he began L'Abri, Dr. Schaeffer preferred to deal with his critics on a private level through careful correspondence and discussion. In this way he hoped he could show the love of Christ for those who disputed his ideas. But he did not carry controversial discussion on for long when he felt the issues and differences of theological opinion had been fully discussed and understood by all parties involved.

8

God Gives Them Growth

Eventually, the Schaeffers' L'Abri became similar to a second-generation China Inland Mission. But God added the new element of making it into *a spiritual orphanage* for wandering young people and adults from all over the world. And with some modifications, it was like a combination of the work of Hudson Taylor and George Müller (the founder of Müller Homes for Children in Bristol, England).[1]

At the beginning, Dr. George H. Seville became their home secretary, and his wife mailed out Edith's family letter about their work to all who were interested. The Sevilles prayed for the Lord to meet all L'Abri's needs, just as they had done for the China Inland Mission. They prayed for the Lord to send the people of His choice to the work: people with questions, as well as workers, helpers, and students.

Dr. Schaeffer maintained a busy schedule by traveling to the University of Lausanne where he met existentialists, humanists, Roman Catholics, liberal Protestants, and many others with a wide variety of philosophical and theological ideas. Two years after they founded L'Abri, Fran began teach-

97

ing medical and university students in Basel, and so many came to Huémoz that they needed to rent Chalet Beau Site to provide a home for the students.

L'Abri never had much money to help the hundreds who came, and by December of 1957 they desperately needed $2,000 to meet their household expenses. In answer to fervent prayer, they received $2,000.35. God usually brought in little amounts day by day to show each visitor and worker that *He* was providing for them. God showed believers and unbelievers alike that He answered prayer, that He provided their home, that He gave them both physical and spiritual food, and they praised Him. God knew who was coming and how to care for each one. God knew which prayers to answer and when to answer them in order to have the greatest positive effect on the greatest number of people—that some might come to saving faith and others have their faith renewed.

In 1958, the Schaeffers began a work in London that later became English L'Abri. And during Christmas break of 1958, students came to Swiss L'Abri from Cambridge, Oxford, and St. Andrews Universities. One of those who came was Ranald Macaulay, who later married their daughter Susan. He became one of the first students at Farel House. He and Susan have now spent more than thirty years of ministry in English L'Abri. An accomplished author, Susan has written books from her father's and mother's perspectives; including *Something Beautiful from God, How to Be Your Own Selfish Pig*, and *For the Children's Sake*.

About the same time the Schaeffers founded L'Abri in Switzerland, a vegetarian Hindu cult was using nearby Chalet les Sapins. Those in L'Abri prayed about the situation and for the people who were being misled by the ideas taught there. They witnessed to the owner several times and tried to show her in practical ways that the true God loved her. Finally, the owner of Chalet les Sapins died. She had stubbornly turned from the Light all around her, so she died with great fears and insecurity. Later, in the 1960s, Chalet les Sapins became a part of L'Abri.

In the early '60s, Fran began speaking all over the world. He spoke at all the major universities and colleges throughout England, Scotland, Wales, Ireland, and the United States. Having debated in college, Fran thought and gave answers quickly. His confidence and courage only improved with constant practice. He presented the case for Christianity reasonably and forcefully.

At Cambridge, he publicly debated a humanist in the midst of a humanist crowd. The crowd thought Fran had won the debate so handily that the humanist was embarrassed. After this "win," Dr. Schaeffer decided never to debate again. He would rather have discussions and try to win the person than have debates and try to win the argument. In speaking of the debate many years later, he said, "Everyone knows that taking the Affirmative Side in a debate, and to speak first, is to take the weakest place. Before the debate, the humanist asked me what side I wanted, and I said, 'Oh, it doesn't matter, you choose.' The humanist decided that I should speak first and take the Affirmative Side. I hated to do it to him, but I simply got up and said briefly, 'I don't have enough faith to believe as the humanist, that everything just came from chance,' and then I sat down. The humanist then spent the rest of the time trying to get out of the box he was in, and he was actually booed by the humanist crowd. I had told all of the Christians to stay away, so the humanists were the ones who did the booing."

Instead of a debate, Dr. Schaeffer participated in a public discussion with the late Bishop James Pike. Bishop Pike taught, with some other liberal theologians, that "God is Dead." Fran tried to show him the love of God as he spoke. After the discussion, Pike wanted to visit with him again. In that later visit, Bishop Pike told him that after he became a Christian he went to a prominent liberal seminary, and there they robbed him of his faith and left him with only "a handful of pebbles." Pike never became a Bible-believing Christian, but Dr. Schaeffer had learned how to discuss and not lose the person, even though the person might still refuse to be won to Christ. The Schaeffers never expected to convert anyone by prayer alone or truth alone. They prayed for unbelievers, but always so they or someone else could teach the truth to them in ways they would accept. The Holy Spirit uses the truth of God and Christians as the means for saving sinners; so God teaches us to pray for the Holy Spirit to do His work in His way in us and others. And when we open our lives to the Holy Spirit's leading, He teaches us whom to pray for, and how to pray for and share the truth with them.

One of the most exciting things about Fran and Edith's work with students in answering their questions was seeing how people from all different walks of life were able to see the reality and the truth of the Bible's answers. This is not to say that

L'Abri was simply an intellectual discussion group. Many hippies came with their drug problems; some came with their minds swimming in clouds of unreality brought on by false philosophies. These people required special care, and many got their thinking cleared up again, accepting Christ as their personal Savior. Some came from the Christian counterculture and did not have a complete understanding of Christian teaching: these believed in Jesus, but their Jesus had no biblical content. Some came saying they had been saved by Jesus, and then went on to say, "but I don't believe in God." In every case, Fran and Edith aimed at speaking and demonstrating the truth by their lives, and at the same time they wanted to show forth the love of God for every person.

Dr. Schaeffer was not immediately successful with every student. In the late 1950s, one student from an English university dismissed Dr. Schaeffer's concerns as "mere intellectualism." Ten years later, after this student began serving on the mission field in Africa, he began struggling for answers to the questions he was being asked. And then Dr. Schaeffer's first books came into his hands. What he had dismissed as "intellectualism" ten years before became the solution to his dilemmas on the mission field of Africa. Born from his work in the mission field of Switzerland, Dr. Schaeffer's work never became "ivory tower theology." His books and ideas remained a practical guide for helping thinking people from all over the world become Christians and live a consistent Christian life.

Dr. Schaeffer kept himself open to the leading of God, and it became obvious to him and others that God wanted him to reach out beyond selected college campuses and the little village of Huémoz to include as many people as possible in gatherings for teaching and answering questions. When asked to lecture or conduct a conference, Dr. Schaeffer did not speak and run; rather, he opened himself to the challenges of other minds—questioning, doubting, searching, and sometimes hostile minds. Sometimes unbelievers attacked him personally and asked hostile questions about Christianity. At other times the questions came from sympathetic listeners seeking understanding and a deeper faith. Fran opened himself to the strict questioning of his ideas, because he believed this was the most compassionate, caring, and non-mechanical way of doing evangelism. He also knew that the Bible and the God he represented could always stand up well in the public forum.

The Schaeffers held the first of many L'Abri conferences at the Ashburnham Conference grounds in England in the spring of 1968. Here 450 people from all walks of life—clergy, students, professors, professionals, laborers, and laypeople—came together for fellowship and discussion. With so many people needing to know L'Abri teachings, but with so many not being able to go to Swiss L'Abri; and with so many people wanting to bring "someone who really needs to hear this" to Dr. Schaeffer, they began to hold these conferences. The overwhelming interest showed Fran that he needed to write more and make his ideas more widely available. Publishers recognized the need and also published Edith's *L'Abri* and other books.

This time was also one of major challenges, as the hippies who came to L'Abri had no concern or compassion for the tiny and very conservative village of Huémoz and the people who saw their way of life being destroyed. After a number of problems, the people of the village and L'Abri came to a mutual recognition of the needs of the young people and the needs of the village. When the Schaeffers moved to Chalet Chardonet in Chesieres, a thirty-minute hike up the hill from Huémoz, and after Fran began his extended speaking tours from their new home, fewer students seemed to inundate the village. Those who came to L'Abri while Fran was away found they could learn from well-educated L'Abri workers and discuss Fran's books and tapes with them. God did not lead Fran away from home until he had prepared others to care for those who came to L'Abri in his absence. L'Abri workers also prayed for God to meet the needs of L'Abri, so the demonstration of God's presence continued whether or not Fran and Edith were there to pray with them.

To understand Fran fully, we must realize that he never sat around "trying to think up 'new theories'" or "theologizing" or "arguing for the sake of arguing" or trying to find "possible answers to possible questions." Instead, he received his training on the front lines of the spiritual battlefield, continuing to learn more beyond his college and seminary education. He talked to real people with real problems and questions from all walks of life. He discovered from his deep involvement with individual human lives (not just from study of the human race theoretically), that most people suffered from the same basic questions and the same basic problems. For these reasons his books have an almost immediate appeal all over the world, with people from a variety of cultures and backgrounds (and especially with non-Christians who consider themselves real thinkers).

Dr. Schaeffer did not thrust himself forward or try to be in the forefront of anything. If he found himself in the forefront, as an evangelist to intellectuals, or as a Protestant advocate of the pro-life cause, it was because God had "extruded him" (one of his favorite phrases when describing how people should look at their developing leadership roles) into that place of prominence at that time. Fran and Edith tried to avoid "lighting their own sparks," and warned others against this too (see Isaiah 50:11).

If you travel to Huémoz, you will see that Dr. Schaeffer really did bury himself and his family in a tiny Swiss village. If God intended this for him, Fran was willing to remain unknown in a small chalet, praying for the Lord to send the people of His choice for him to help, helping only a few people. He really did not want to administer a large and growing work in Huémoz or in other branches, and that was not his final calling. God gave Fran His own love and understanding for His people around the world, for people who could not go to that little chalet in Switzerland for help. Then God enabled him to reach out to these people through books and tapes. And all the while, God sent L'Abri new leaders who could do the administrative tasks, provide counseling, and teach. His three daughters entered into (and continue) in the work of L'Abri with their husbands. John and Priscilla Sandri still teach in Swiss L'Abri, and John bears heavy administrative burdens. Ranald and Susan Macaulay work in English L'Abri, teaching students and writing. Udo and Debbie Middelmann direct and teach in the Francis Schaeffer Foundation in New York.[2] Some of Fran and Edith's grandchildren work in L'Abri or with other missionary groups.

Dr. Schaeffer's first books were published because reprints of his talks were soon demanded by those who heard him and wanted others to learn about his ideas. His talks to American college students became *The God Who Is There*. Other lectures became *Escape From Reason*, which was published about the same time. These two books, along with *He Is There and He Is Not Silent* became the Schaeffer trilogy. He compared these three books to the hub of a wheel. The Schaeffer trilogy is the middle hub, and books such as *Death in the City* are spokes from the wheel because they are a practical application of the three foundational books. The trilogy became Schaeffer's foundation for showing how the Christian faith relates to every aspect of human life. Fran received letters from everywhere about his first two books, even from the president of Senegal.

His radio talks began in December 1971 through the Trans-World Radio Station in Monte Carlo. These broadcasts reached all over Europe, into Russia behind the Iron Curtain, and into the Near East and North Africa. Recorded in a tiny office later used by John Sandri (the husband of Priscilla), the talks brought more people to L'Abri, and some of these talks became books. The books enabled people to share Dr. Schaeffer's ideas in ways that could not have been possible otherwise. Before and after his death, a group of twenty-five wives of U.S. Congressmen met every Friday morning to study systematically his and Edith's books. His twenty-one books have sold in the millions, and they have been translated into at least twenty-four languages. When the family moved to Rochester, Minnesota, they were amazed to pack at least 126 first editions of his books in various translations.

Dr. Schaeffer became actively involved in formal theological education by becoming a visiting lecturer at Covenant Theological Seminary in St. Louis and at the Theological Academy in Basel, Switzerland. These times of lecturing away from home gave people who could not study for a prolonged time at Farel House in Huémoz the opportunity to think deeply and discuss openly with him how they could apply the Gospel of Jesus Christ to the whole of life.

Dr. Schaeffer was welcomed not only at evangelical colleges, but also at most of the major Ivy League universities in America. In 1968 he spoke at Harvard, in 1972 he spoke at Princeton, and in 1973 he spoke at Yale. In those days, it was unusual to have large crowds worship in the Princeton University Chapel on Sundays, but when Fran spoke the 2,500-seat sanctuary was packed. Later, some of the university students went to the Princeton Seminary bookstore for books on apologetics (the rational defense of the Christian faith), but there were few to be found. Fran's books and lectures were truly needed at this time.

In addition to these American universities, he lectured at Helsinki University, Lund University, the Chinese University, Hong Kong University, and the University of Malaya. On June 12, 1971, Gordon College awarded Fran the honorary Doctor of Letters degree. He also spoke to various groups in Washington, D.C., to White House workers in the Ford, Carter, and Reagan administrations, to members of Congress and their families, and to other government workers. For the last fifteen years of his ministry, he always had an open door for ministry among U.S. government leaders.

Fran had extensive influence in government and university circles for several reasons. He took a biblical, rational, practical, prayerful, and compassionate approach to the Christian faith. The rational approach convinced those who lived on the cutting edge of human life to accept the Bible as true and Christ as Savior. While he answered people's questions, he also prayed for those who needed answers for reality, who needed a foundation for making the right decisions—decisions that would affect millions of people in government, education, and business. Dr. Schaeffer understood modern man and the foundations of his ideas and actions. He did not appeal to people's selfishness or self-interest by telling them to accept Christ for all that He could do for them. Rather, he knew that conversion to Christ involves turning from self-centeredness to Christ-centeredness, to putting the claims of Jesus Christ first in one's life. He presented Christianity as *the only viable option that is true to reality* and then he demanded that people live on the basis of Christian truth.

9

Fighting the Good Fight

In 1974 Dr. Schaeffer addressed the Lausanne
Congress on World Evangelization and declared
that the church today must emphasize Christian
holiness, purity of life, and purity of doctrine.
Christians must realize the reality of God and the
supernatural in the midst of this present life, and
this cannot be forgotten as they try to do evangelism. "Evangelism that does not lead to purity of life
and purity of doctrine is just as faulty and incom-
plete as an orthodoxy which does not lead to a concern for, and communication with, the lost."[1]

Dr. Schaeffer taught that the inerrancy of Scripture is the watershed issue for Bible-believing
churches. The watershed is that place where water
runs off the mountain and then goes down one side
or the other. Churches either move toward God or
away from God based upon affirming or denying
that the Bible is true in all that it affirms, including
the areas where it touches history. If *believing the
Bible is true* is the first step to saving faith, then it
can be seen that once the inerrancy of Scripture is
given up, disastrous consequences will follow: for
one by one the essential Christian doctrines will be
questioned and begin to fall in the doubting mind.

But if conservative and evangelical churches return to their historic and *truly biblical* position on the authority and the inerrancy of Scripture, then what the apostle Paul wrote would be true in their midst and make them more effective:

> Then we will no longer be infants, tossed back and forth by the waves, and blown here and there by every wind of teaching and the cunning and craftiness of men in their deceitful scheming. Instead, *speaking the truth in love*, we will in all things grow up into him who is the Head, that is, Christ. From him the whole body, joined and held together by every supporting ligament, grows and builds itself up in love, as each part does its work. So I tell you this, and insist on it in the Lord, that you must no longer live as the Gentiles do, in the futility of their thinking (Ephesians 4:14–17).

Dr. Schaeffer emphasized that concern for the purity of the church should not lead to the hatred, bitterness, and unloveliness that had characterized his experiences in the '40s and '50s. He pleaded for truth. But as he always endeavored to speak the truth in love, he called for others to make love their aim as they spoke the truth of God. This cannot be done in the flesh, but only in the power of the indwelling Holy Spirit; therefore, Fran built his life and work on prayer in a moment-by-moment communication with God. And he insisted that all believers should do the same.

Often Fran discussed the problems of Bible-believing Christians who stayed in the liberal denominations in hopes of bearing their witness.[2] He remembered how some Bible-believing Christians, who felt called to leave, treated those who stayed. He emphasized that Bible-believing Christians should not separate from one another, but they should support one another in the truth and love of the Lord. His advice to those struggling about what to do included: "I am not the Holy Spirit. I cannot be the Holy Spirit for anyone. You must pray about these things and seek the Lord's leading. The Holy Spirit can call some to stay in these denominations, and He can call others out." On the other hand, he also added, "I know for myself that I could never have accomplished what I have for the Lord if I had stayed in and had tried to fight the battles from the inside."

When various leaders and pastors from a variety of denominations came to him for advice, he noted that in recent history only one mainline denomination had fought the battle for the Bible in their church and won against the liberals. In some other denominations the battle had yet to be decided. His observations led him to warn that when the denomination's bureaucracy or leadership and the seminaries have been captured by the theological liberals the battle is lost. Liberals always tended to infiltrate, subvert, and take over institutions from the inside. With the possible exception of the World Council of Churches, he observed that liberals have never created a major theological institution (they have always taken them from the Bible-believing Christians).

To help Christians learn that in the battles we face we must always speak the truth in love, he wrote *The Church Before the Watching World*. He cried when he learned that his teachings in that book had helped many Bible-believing Christians maintain fellowship one with another although they might be in different denominations. Dr. Schaeffer believed that if we hold to the essentials of the Christian faith, then we have a large circle of people (who also hold to the essentials) with whom we can cooperate and have fellowship even though they may be in churches of other denominations. Still, he insisted strongly that those who stay in the theologically liberal denominations cannot accommodate the liberals, but must continue to confront them with love in all areas of truth, in practice, and doctrine.

In 1974, Dr. Schaeffer also began to work on a new project—a project that marked a turning point in the lives of many people. Leaders and teachers in L'Abri began working together on the book and film series *How Should We Then Live?* Filmed in Germany, Switzerland, France, Italy, England, Holland, Belgium, and the United States, the filming took six months to complete. It has been translated into several languages. The book and film were written in response to Kenneth Clark's book *Civilisation*. Clark was an atheist, though he seemed to believe that Eastern religious thought was the pinnacle of man's religious reaching for spiritual enlightenment. His book took a definite anti-Christian stance, and his film series from the book was aired widely over public television.

Though made without the immense financial backing given *Civilisation*, Dr. Schaeffer's book and film were the best Christian response to Clark and others who taught that Christianity is the enemy of intellectual endeavors and achievements. As Schaeffer's work swept over the whole of Western intellectual life and thought, many realized for the

first time that Christianity *did* have the intellectual answers to the philosophical questions—questions that had been raised on the university level
and not solved on the seminary level or in the
churches of the day. Many saw that the liberal seminaries left unanswered or refused to address the
basic philosophical questions, but the Bible did and
the Bible gave the right answers. While watching
one of the ten episodes, a theologically liberal pastor was converted to Bible-believing Christianity
and said afterwards, "Now all the pieces fit together! My Christian faith used to be just a jumble
of puzzle pieces, of truths and errors that did not fit
together with the world as it is. For the first time I
can see the beautiful picture of Christian truth. The
puzzle has been put together, I see how everything
fits!"[3]

   How Should We Then Live? showed what Dr.
Schaeffer struggled with in all of his books: "To
make a reality day by day of the lordship of Christ
in the whole of life, in the area of culture as well as
all else . . . to broaden the reality of honestly exhib-
iting the lordship of Christ in regard to social issues
and political life, medicine (human life), and government."[4] For this reason, and because of the
scope of his works, *The Complete Works of Francis
A. Schaeffer* is subtitled *A Christian Worldview*. In
1982, Schaeffer completely revised his books and
added new appendices to some. His *Complete Works*
show not only the full scope of his learning but also
why he was able to give to the world a new respect
for the names "fundamentalist" or "evangelical."
By the time *The Complete Works* was completed,
however, some evangelical churches' teachings
were in such disarray and some of them so anti-bib-

lical that Fran chose to call himself a "Bible-believing Christian," and talk about "Bible-believing Christianity," but as one person remarked, "Can there really be any other kind of Christianity?"

The intellectual integrity of Bible-believing Christianity really began to make an impact upon the masses and swept across the American continent when the Schaeffers led the first seminar for the film series *How Should We Then Live?* in January 1977, with 5,500 people attending. But Satan retaliated against them, and L'Abri felt his flaming arrows. During the seminars, Edith's father died. Hans Rookmaaker, who had worked so hard on the film series, also died unexpectedly. The chapel in Huémoz burned and its beautiful organ was almost destroyed. It appeared that Satan intended to attack the Schaeffers from many sides all at once. But what Satan meant for evil, God turned to good. Fran and Edith were well aware of how Satan's sharp arrows could inflict much suffering, and Edith has said, "Satan so often attacks in ways that the Lord turns into something powerful in counterattack."[5] Satan did not want *How Should We Then Live?* to have an impact on his kingdom of darkness. But with every attack, the Schaeffers and L'Abri demonstrated the truth of their teachings in the whole of life and gave their teachings even more credibility. They proved, even as Job proved, that believers in God will not forsake Him and run in the midst of persecution. They proved the value and strength of biblical faith in times of persecution. They intensified their efforts on God's behalf, and began to attack Satan's kingdom on more than one front.

Many answers to prayer sustained the Schaeffers and L'Abri during these very difficult times. God moved some people to send extra money, and new workers volunteered their efforts. The book and film series had a remarkable effect upon Western culture and Christian leaders in various governments around the world. From a historical perspective, *How Should We Then Live?* warned the churches and Western governments of coming dangers, and Dr. Schaeffer became one of the "watchmen who saw the sword coming and blew the trumpet" (see Ezekiel 33:1–19). He did so by using the best medium that he could use, a contemporary film series.

As Dr. Schaeffer rested from writing his book, filming the series, and conducting a seminar tour, he heard of Dr. C. Everett Koop's series of meetings at Swiss L'Abri. He became convinced that he and Dr. Koop should write a book and do a film, *Whatever Happened to the Human Race?* This film series on abortion, infanticide, and euthanasia rocked the Western world and brought vehement protests and even death threats to the Schaeffers. Others praised their efforts, including President Ronald Reagan and some in the English Parliament, for awakening the Protestant conscience to the central moral issue of the time. Dr. Schaeffer brought a new biblical and intellectual integrity to Christian social involvement.

Many viewers expressed amazement as the film spoke of *the possibility* of infanticide "in the future." But at the film seminars, time and again clergy and medical people testified about children being starved to death recently in nearby hospitals. Some children were starved on purpose simply because their handicap would inconvenience their parents as they grew. Some children only needed minor surgery, that a "normal" baby would have received. Seminar participants learned from each other. Many expressed shock upon hearing about some doctors and ministers who had worked together and counseled parents to let their babies with Down syndrome starve to death in the hospital, rather than correct an intestinal blockage (a simple procedure). Regarding the treatment of the elderly, some ministers testified they had been present when doctors said bluntly, "Society has a concern here," as they pressured families to decide to terminate the feeding of their loved ones. These ministers struggled to overcome the devastating effects of such "medical advice" upon the family. In the film series, Dr. Schaeffer predicted that if people do not turn back to faith in Jesus Christ and live on a biblical basis, then we will face doctor-assisted suicide and the elimination of anyone who has problems or pain or seems "unfit to live."

The film series raised issues that Christians and others needed to discuss. Some evangelical churches didn't want to disrupt their evangelical programs or "rock their boats," and so they tried to ignore the issues that Dr. Schaeffer and Dr. C. Everett Koop, later U.S. Surgeon General, made in the films. Many others, however, did listen. Perhaps millions more will listen to the call to save lives and to change laws in those countries that allow the civil rights of unborn children to be violated by their mothers who have abortions by doctors who murder children for hire. Abortion in America is a multimillion-dollar business, with 476 abortions being performed for every 1,000 live births. Powerful forces work to continue these brutal murders.

In the eyes of God, abortion is murder and a violation of the Ten Commandments and the Law of Love. Under the guise of population control, some abortion advocates even argue that to preserve the human race we need to kill as many of our unborn children as possible. No wonder the film asks, *Whatever Happened to the Human Race?*

During 1977, when satanic attacks seemed to be at their height and a new project to save humanity had begun, Edith Schaeffer wrote the book *Affliction*. Perhaps her most important book, she finished it by October 2, 1977. One year later, the Schaeffers traveled to Mayo Clinic in Rochester, Minnesota. Here they learned that Dr. Schaeffer had an advanced case of cancer called lymphoma. Some doctors thought he had only six weeks to six months to live. Edith believed that God inspired her to write *Affliction* and gave it to them as well as to others to help sustain them over the years ahead. Many pastors and counselors found in her book real answers for afflicted, sick, and dying people. *Affliction* gave needed answers from a whole biblical perspective, rather than a fragmented, non-Christian perspective. It has blessed many who have needed to read a biblical interpretation of their own personal suffering.

When fighting for truth, biblical values, sound doctrine, true faith in Jesus Christ, holiness and love, the lives of others and his own life, Fran intended to obey these commands of the apostle Paul: "Fight the good fight of the faith. Take hold of the eternal life to which you were called when you made your good confession in the presence of many witnesses" (1 Timothy 6:12). And whenever he

looked toward the close of his life, he wanted to be
able to say, along with Paul: "I have fought the good
fight, I have finished the race, I have kept the faith"
(2 Timothy 4:7).

10

From Strength to Strength

Dr. C. Everett Koop and Francis Schaeffer began filming *Whatever Happened to the Human Race?* in August 1978. On September 18, 1978, they had filmed the scene on the shore of Galilee about the risen Christ. Of that fifth episode in the series, Dr. Schaeffer said, "It is the best presentation of the Gospel I have ever been able to make." On the final day of shooting the film in October, they discovered that Fran's coat no longer fit. He had lost more than twenty-five pounds, was exhausted, and breathed with difficulty. Edith started the preparations to get Dr. Schaeffer to the hospital.

On Tuesday, October 10, 1978, the Schaeffers met their friends, Dr. Victor Wahby and Dr. Carl Morlock, at the Rochester airport in Minnesota. Dr. Robert M. Petitt began treatment for lymphoma on October 17. The doctors had found a tumor the size of a football.

Dr. Schaeffer's cancer went into remission at least twice in answer to prayer and in response to the excellent medical treatment of Mayo Clinic and the nutritional foods provided by Edith. The Schaeffers saw no inconsistency between receiving medical attention, a gift from God as a part of the battle in this fallen world, and believing God could heal. Medicine and faithful prayer go together, and God empowered Dr. Schaeffer to live five more years instead of six weeks, because He had more work for Fran to do.

Dr. Schaeffer did amazing things for Christ and the world while he fought for his life. He continued to walk three miles a day, as often as he was able. The strong heart he had acquired from his many hikes in the Alps, from chopping wood for the wood stoves in the chalets, and from his gardening and landscaping work outdoors as he visited with L'Abri students, prepared him physically to withstand the damaging effect of chemotherapy as it attacked both the good and bad cells in his body. He looked upon his walks as quiet times to pray and be with the Lord in the beautiful world God had made.

By January 1979, in Rochester, Fran began to speak to various groups of doctors and hospital chaplains. He showed the complete series of *How Should We Then Live?* to a full auditorium at the John Marshall High School in Rochester. After having chemotherapy in the morning, he answered questions on almost every subject in the evening. Many listeners became convinced of the sufficiency of the Bible's answers to the questions life poses.

Even during the early months of his treatments, people continued to come into his home with questions as they sought to find the reality in Christian teachings. Some came seeking the faith that had been stolen from them by their liberal churches and pastors. Some came right after his chemotherapy treatment; he did not mention this inconvenience but put their needs first. He would not have been able to do this if he had not practiced this way of ministry throughout his life. Often, as he sat in a waiting room at Mayo Clinic, people recognized him and asked if he was Dr. Schaeffer. Then they expressed warm words of appreciation for his books and films, or asked deep and perplexing questions as he waited to see the doctors or take a chemotherapy treatment. He made himself accessible to people, and he never stopped praying every day, "Lord, send the people of *your* choice to me today." No matter what they themselves suffered, Fran and Edith looked upon every person who came to them as a person sent directly from God.

Fran helped many people in Rochester, and Edith often opened their home for crowds of people to come for questions and answers on various evenings, even after Fran had spent the day writing, visiting with individuals, or seeing doctors. One young girl he helped was struggling to free herself from a local cult. She wrote Dr. Schaeffer a letter, and he called her on the phone in response. His compassionate care and sound advice gave her the strength to make the final break from the cult and throw the cult's books and materials in the trash. She returned to her family and church, and then began to serve others on the basis of Fran's books and films.

Dr. and Mrs. Schaeffer were accessible to almost everyone at all times, but that does not mean this was an easy choice for them to make. Fran suffered silently from his illness, and as he tried to help others he never complained to them or put his own needs before theirs. The Holy Spirit gave him the strength to make the needs of others his complete focus of attention for the time that was required. He called on patients in the Rochester hospitals, continuing the work of a simple pastor, never thinking he was better than anyone else or too great to give others his time. In a speech to the hospital chaplains he said that he was glad he had something to say in the midst of the absurdity of cancer and the other horrible diseases that people suffer. He said, "I can go talk to patients and tell them, 'God hates your cancer.' And I am encouraged when I remember that at the tomb of Lazarus 'Jesus wept,' and Jesus could weep and be angry at death, even though He was God. He could be angry at death, and not be angry at himself as the Creator."

Dr. Schaeffer knew this is a fallen world, and he had something to say because his faith was firmly grounded on the content of the Bible. He could help people act in faith upon the total unified Christian teaching of God's Word. He could remind people that we live in a supernatural universe—that ever since the rebellion of man we face a battle. This battle is in the seen and the unseen world. And so he encouraged people to be contented before God and yet fight the battle against their diseases and other afflictions.

Throughout his own long suffering, Fran maintained contentment before the Lord. He maintained a quiet disposition and gave thanks to God for His love to him. His trust in his heavenly Father had been built up over more than fifty years of serving Him, so when times were their darkest for him personally his trust in God never faltered. He talked to God as people talk to their own earthly fathers, and in times of trouble asked God, "What do you want me to learn from this?" The special hospital ministry that Fran began in Rochester is still carried on by Rochester L'Abri.

In the summer of 1979, L'Abri held the first of two Rochester Conferences. Satan's attacks upon the Schaeffers only increased the usefulness of their ministry and demonstrated more effectively than otherwise possible the character and power of the God who is there. Almost two thousand people attended their first conference, coming from forty-seven of the fifty states. Dr. Schaeffer insisted during the conference planning meetings that the motivation for all advertising must be compassion, compassion for those who really needed to hear about the conference so they could be helped. For many Rochester residents, and for others attending a L'Abri conference for the first time, the various members of L'Abri who spoke showed the depth of knowledge and understanding that the leaders in every branch of L'Abri possess. God had truly led the people of His choice into the work over the years. The work would be ably carried on, even if Fran died. In between the workers' lectures, they gave themselves totally to answering the questions of many troubled people. They didn't even have time to hear one another speak.

Dr. Schaeffer wanted to help as many hurting people as he could, with the short time he had left. He was not making up for lost time, because he had always served the Lord completely. He did not seek glory for himself: he had already died to seeking personal glory when he buried himself in the Swiss Alps and began L'Abri. He remained humble before the Lord, authentic through and through, and the Lord raised him up and honored him. When someone praised him, he simply said, "Well, I am grateful," for he was grateful that God had used him to help someone else. He lived to honor God and lead people to accept Jesus Christ as their Lord and Savior, making Him the Lord of all life. He strived to help all people be of help to others on the basis of the truth of Scripture and the finished work of Christ.

In September 1979, the seminars for *Whatever Happened to the Human Race?* began in Philadelphia and moved from East to West. Later, Minnesota Citizens Concerned for Life and other such groups bought the film series and made it available for pro-life causes around the country. On January 22, 1981, Minnesota Governor Al Quie honored Dr. Schaeffer at a special dinner at the governor's mansion in St. Paul and thanked him for his work in the pro-life movement.

Dr. Schaeffer did more than just write against abortion. On a Wednesday afternoon, October 26, 1983, he led a silent, dignified march of six people in front of the Methodist Hospital in Rochester, Minnesota, to protest against the hospital and some of the Mayo Clinic doctors who performed abortions there. He wanted to show that we cannot always wait until we can get hundreds together to do something important. He proved that a small group with carefully worded placards can make a quiet and orderly statement for the lives of unborn children. Three men and three women dressed neatly in business suits carried six signs bearing a unified message: "This hospital is normally committed to saving human life, but abortion reverses this; abortion is the killing of a human life; abortion devaluates the unique value of all human life; it is the value of everyone's life that is involved; abortion is the killing of a human life." At the conclusion of the march, Dr. Schaeffer told reporters what he had said so often: "What they ought to realize is that they are schizophrenic. A policy of healing and the practice of abortion on demand are contradictory."[1] Some who passed the hospital that day said they had not known that Mayo Clinic doctors performed abortions there. Others in some stores nearby mocked and asked, "Who is that old man leading that march?"

With *How Should We Then Live?* Dr. Schaeffer demonstrated the necessity of the biblical Christian answers as the foundation for living. He showed the intellectual substance of biblical Christian faith when compared to other ideas and philosophies. In *Whatever Happened to the Human Race?* he emphasized the necessity of moral absolutes based upon the Bible. He carried the application of personal faith to the next logical step: to social action based upon the moral absolutes and principles that could be derived from the Bible.

God kept Dr. Schaeffer alive during twenty strenuous seminars for *Whatever Happened to the Human Race?* By February 1980 the cancer was back in full force again, but he did not stop. He went to the White House to talk with Christian leaders, and while in Washington he conducted another seminar of *Whatever Happened to the Human Race?* with other government leaders. This seminar, along with much other work by many people, gave intellectual vigor and moral strength to those in Congress and in the White House who are in favor of protecting human beings of all ages.

After speaking in America, Dr. Schaeffer crossed the Atlantic for more seminars in England.

Dr. Koop and an English doctor held discussions with him. These efforts almost single-handedly caused a radical change of opinion in much of England regarding the sanctity of human life. Later, Malcolm Muggeridge, Mother Teresa, and others joined Dr. Schaeffer at Hyde Park, where fifty thousand people rallied to promote the sanctity of human life and then marched to Trafalgar Square. In this case, thousands made a difference and Parliament worked to make changes.

L'Abri had moved its American headquarters to Rochester in 1979, so Dr. Schaeffer would also have work when he came for his medical treatments. They held discussions on Monday nights in their home, and the crowds grew so large that they needed to meet in the Plummer House, a mansion built by the late Dr. Henry Plummer of Mayo Clinic and then donated to the City of Rochester. People from a great variety of intellectual backgrounds and interests, Christians as well as non-Christians, profited from these discussions. Many who came did not realize Dr. Schaeffer was often in the midst of chemotherapy treatments. Over and over again the doctors told him, "Now everyone gets *really* sick from this type of chemical," but over and over again his heavenly Father surprised them at how well he did. He did have times of great tiredness, depression, intense pain, and other complications, but through it all God showed His gentle and compassionate character.

On some occasions church groups from various denominations traveled to see him at his home in Rochester to ask advice on how they could fight the battle for truth within their denomination. At other times he spoke at large denominational meetings and warned of the theological dangers they faced. Because Dr. Schaeffer was a Presbyterian minister, he had his own distinctive reformation view of the sacraments and other matters. But Baptists, Lutherans, and others knew that he would not get off into denominational distinctives and push his views in a public debate at their meetings. They trusted Dr. Schaeffer to help them fight for the truth in the essential places where the battles needed to take place. For this reason, most Bible-believing churches welcomed him gladly as a speaker, and he had more requests to speak than he could possibly fulfill.

Dr. Schaeffer had the gift of fighting where the battle should take place and of keeping peace where there should be peace among Bible-believing Christians and their churches. When he edited his *Complete Works*, he made certain that it included biblical views that all Bible-believing Christians should agree upon, and for this reason his books have been used by a broad spectrum of Bible-believing Christians and different denominations.

Dr. Schaeffer could have quit after his seminars for *Whatever Happened to the Human Race?*, but the seminars only reinforced for him the necessity of continued fighting in other crucial areas. He would say, "How can I think of retiring at a time like this!" Fran began to fight harder for freedom of religion and freedom of speech in governments that suppressed the truth. But the battle also needed to be fought in America, as some have tried to systematically shut out Christianity and religious ideas in the schools and other institutions. It seemed as though the United States and the Soviet Union had something in common: in neither country could a person acknowledge the existence of God in the classroom! Thankfully, as of today, people can acknowledge God publicly in Russia, and Dr. Schaeffer's son-in-law, Udo Middelmann, can preach and teach there. But only a little headway has been made in allowing Americans to practice their faith in the ways of the nation's founders. Dr. Schaeffer faced the fact that Christians were being denied their First-Amendment rights of free speech and assembly, simply because they were Christians! He encouraged the founding of Christian schools. Along with other members of his family, he encouraged Christians who wanted to home school.

As part of his battle for religious freedom in America, Fran wrote the best seller *A Christian Manifesto*. He wept for his Christian brothers and sisters in the Eastern bloc, people who had to pay a real price for their convictions. He prayed that some radicals would not take his ideas and twist them and use them in wrong ways in the name of Christ. Because of his work in this area, in 1983 he received the honorary Doctor of Laws Degree from Simon Greenleaf School of Law.

In his last years, Fran also wept when he had to fight for the truth and authority of the Bible in the churches that claimed to be evangelical or conservative. Having lived through the liberal takeover of the churches in the early '30s, he understood far too well that many of the younger evangelicals were selling out in their eagerness to accommodate new liberal forces. He knew how easily false ideas could infiltrate minds and churches. He had warned and saved many evangelical churches from Barthianism in the 1950s, and now he had to warn a new generation of pastors and theologians. So, shortly before his death, he wrote *The Great Evangelical Disaster*, much of which he proofread from his hospital bed. One month before Dr. Schaeffer died, God gave him strength to complete a thirteen-seminar tour on his book. Those who knew him saw God give him supernatural strength to do His will the last six months of his life, as he had to get the message of *The Great Evangelical Disaster* into churches and college campuses. He prayed that Christians, and especially pastors, would uphold the truth of God's Word in their churches—no matter what the personal cost—for the sake of the truth and the next generation.

Dr. Schaeffer saw all these efforts as the practice of "true spirituality," and that is why he was particularly pleased after he reworked *True Spirituality* in his *Complete Works*. This book effectively opens the door to understanding him and the practical application of Christian faith. It laid out the foundation for all of his subsequent work. It explained the centrality of personal Christian experience based upon the objective truth of the Bible and the finished work of Christ on the Cross. It insisted that believers need to love others and be involved in the whole of life on the basis of love and truth.

By April 1984, Dr. Schaeffer was so exhausted he could hardly move. He spent Easter Sunday in the cancer ward at St. Mary's Hospital while doctors thought about possible treatments and fought for his life, trying to find just the right formula that might turn the tide once again. But Dr. Schaeffer could not remember when he had ever been so tired. He looked forward to living his final days with Edith in their home not far from the hospital and near the other L'Abri homes. He was intrigued about what work God would have him do now, but at the same time he wanted to go be with Jesus. On one occasion he said, "One of these days I am going to go to sleep and not wake up." He showed no fear. At other times, he reminded those nearby about the importance of spreading the Word of God, of upholding the truth of the Bible, of loving one another, of fighting for human life. He knew that Jesus had prepared a place for him, and sometimes he prayed for Jesus to take him home; yet he, like the apostle Paul, wanted to stay for the sake of others.

Fran never gave up. As he neared death, he remarked, "I have felt the power and the authority of God in my life over these past five years. By God's grace, I have been able to do more in these last five years than in all the years before I had cancer." Dr. Schaeffer was needed as a Christian public figure in America to demonstrate that no matter what the battle, we can "keep on, keeping on," and never give up. He insisted that in fighting an illness we are not fighting God or God's will for our lives. There is no inconsistency between taking medicine and praying for healing. Taking medicine is not a sign of a lack of faith, and being sick is not a sign of lack of faith either.

The Word of God sustained his faith, and one of the Scriptures that encouraged him most was Psalm 84, verses 5–7: "Blessed are those whose strength is in you, who have set their hearts on pilgrimage. As they pass through the Valley of Baca [Valley of Weeping], they make it a place of springs; the autumn rains also cover it with pools. *They go from strength to strength* till each appears before God in Zion" (emphasis added). Dr. Schaeffer went "from strength to strength" several times during his battle against cancer, and when he went to meet the Lord at the end of his faithful pilgrimage, he went on "from strength to strength." After his faithful pilgrimage on this earth, through his books and Edith's accounts of their lives, he has kept on giving people springs of "living water" to drink.

The doctors finally said there was nothing else they could do. One option was to put him into an intensive care unit, where his family could visit only briefly every few hours. Another option was simply to let him stay in his hospital room. The option they chose was to let him go home to be with his family among the familiar surroundings of the furnishings Edith had hurriedly brought from their old home in Switzerland in order to provide a place of continuity in the midst of change. Edith told him gently, "We are traveling on different roads together, roads that neither of us has ever traveled before." He went to their new home knowing he had but a short time left with his wife and family. But he went home still fighting for his life. A few days before he died, Mayo Clinic doctors went to his home with one more dose of chemotherapy. He told them quietly, "Thank you for fighting."

Nurses who later attended him at home continually marveled at how much support his own family gave him in his illness. Some had never seen such support from a family before. They saw Christian faith make a real difference. Even in their most difficult hours, the Schaeffers testified to the substantial reality we can have with our heavenly Father through faith in Jesus Christ.

Dr. Schaeffer died early in the morning of May 15, 1984. He left quietly to be with the Lord, and the Lord encouraged his family with an appropriate message that He knew they would read from *Daily Light*, the reading for that very day. Debbie brought it to the attention of the family, and it was read at his funeral in Rochester and again at a simple graveside service one year later to encourage his family and close friends to "keep on."

On a bright and beautiful day, May 20, 1984, as more than eight hundred people crowded the auditorium of the John Marshall High School, the site of his two L'Abri Conferences and other meetings, Dr. Schaeffer's fifth episode of *Whatever Happened to the Human Race?* was shown. Here, at his funeral service, he could speak through a film on the value, meaning, and power for us of the Resurrection of Jesus Christ. People turned their eyes with faith toward God as they watched Dr. Schaeffer speak before the empty tomb of Jesus Christ or by a simple fishing boat on the shore of the Sea of Galilee. Many wept as they listened to these words from *Daily Light* that Debbie had read to the family on the very day he died:

> *He will wipe every tear from their eyes. There will be no more death or mourning or crying or pain, for the old order of things has passed away.*
>
> He will swallow up death forever ... The Sovereign Lord will wipe away the tears from all faces; he will remove the disgrace of his people from all the earth. The Lord has spoken. . . . No one living in Zion will say, "I am ill"; and the sins of those who dwell there will be forgiven. . . . The sound of weeping and of crying will be heard in it no more. . . . Sorrow and

sighing will fly away.

I will ransom them from the power of the grave; I will redeem them from death. Where, O death, are your plagues? Where, O grave, is your destruction? The last enemy to be destroyed is death. . . . Then the saying that is written will come true: "Death has been swallowed up in victory."

What is unseen is eternal.

God raised us up with Christ.

"Do not be afraid. . . . I am the living One." "Father, I want those you have given me to be with me where I am."

For we are members of his body. And he is the head of the body, the church; he is the beginning and the firstborn from among the dead. . . . You have been given fullness in Christ, who is the head over every power and authority.

Since the children have flesh and blood, he too shared in their humanity so that by his death he might destroy him who holds the power of death—that is, the devil—and free those who all their lives were held in slavery by their fear of death.

For the perishable must clothe itself with the imperishable, and the mortal with immortality. When the perishable has been clothed with the imperishable, the mortal with immortality, then the saying that is written will come true: "Death has been swallowed up in victory."[2]

Is the Bible just words? Are these particular words "only a positive statement in the midst of an absurd situation"? No! A thousand times, no! God is there! God has not been and is not silent! God has spoken! God's Word is perfect, and often given to us with perfect timing. When a Christian dies, there is an eternal difference; he knows that through Christ his sins are forgiven, and that he goes to a place Jesus has prepared for him. When Christians who are left behind say "goodbye" to a loved one who they know will go to be with the Lord, the fact that God has spoken *truly* makes all the difference.

Regarding Francis Schaeffer's journey to be face to face with his great Friend, Jesus Christ, Edith wrote about the day of his death on May 15:

> It was at 4:00 A.M. precisely that a soft last breath was taken . . . and he was absent. That absence was so sharp and precise! Absent. Now I only observed the absence. I can vouch for the absence being precisely at 4:00 A.M. . . . as can Debbie and Sue, and Shirley, the nurse (a L'Abri person from Canada). As for his presence with the Lord . . . I had to turn to my BIBLE to know that. I only know that a person is present with the Lord because the *Bible* tells us so. I did not have a mystical experience. I want to tell you here and now that the inerrant Bible became more important to me than ever before. I want to tell you very seriously and solemnly . . . the Bible is more precious than ever to me. My husband fought for truth and fought for the truth of the inspiration of the Bible— the inerrancy of the Bible—all the days that I knew him . . . through my 52 years of knowing him. But—never have I been more impressed with the wonder of having a trustworthy message from God, an unshakable word from God—than right then! I did not have to have, nor pretend to have, some mystical experience to prove that Fran had left to go somewhere . . .

that he had gone TO the prepared place for him, and that he was indeed OK. I could know that by turning to my precious Bible, and to his precious Bible (and we each have had several), and read again that absent from the body is present with the Lord . . . and that is far better. It is far better for the one who is thus present— but not for those left behind. God knows all about the pain of separation . . . and is preparing that separation will be over forever one future day. I also know that because the Bible tells me so. I feel very sorry for the people who have to be "hoping without any assurance" . . . because they *don't know* what portion of the Bible is myth and what portion might possibly be trusted. What fear must clutch their hearts as the face of their loved one suddenly turns to wax after the last breath announces the absence!![3]

Following Schaeffer's death, President Ronald Reagan wrote these words to comfort his family: "He will long be remembered as one of the great Christian thinkers of our century." And Dr. Billy Graham commended Fran as "truly one of the great evangelical statesmen of our generation."

11

An Unfolding Rose

Following Fran's death, Edith continued to unfold as a beautiful red rose facing the sun and inspiring others with its radiant beauty. Though she grieved the personal loss of her husband, she too "kept on keeping on," and looked for new ways to serve the Lord in Fran's absence. As she worked without Fran, God allowed others to see better her God-given gifts. Over the subsequent years, many widows have been inspired by Edith's courage and strength. Her daily devotional book, *The Art of Life*, with the unfolding rose on each personal notes page shows that Christians can continue to grow spiritually and bless others no matter what their physical limitations or afflictions.

As this last chapter is being written, Edith Schaeffer remains snowbound in New York City, slogging through the "Great Blizzard of '96." Though 81 years old, people still want to hear her speak and discuss her books. Because of the snow, she has cancelled three speaking engagements, but she hopes to speak later at The Francis A. Schaeffer Foundation in New York. Friends of Fran and Edith helped create the Schaeffer Foundation, and Debbie Schaeffer Middelmann and Udo Middelmann oversee the work. Edith still works hard. For her eightieth birthday present, she traveled back to her home in China and met some who became Christians through the China Inland Mission. Twelve years have passed since the death of her husband, and she has carried on their work with the talents and tireless energy God gives her. The mighty waters often rose as they fought together, especially in Fran's last years, but they continued in prayer and God sustained her faith through Fran's illness and after his death. For more than thirty years, the Schaeffers and L'Abri have demonstrated God's power through prayer to overcome Satan in all things and to glorify God.

By His Spirit, God often gives widows or widowers more opportunities to serve Him, and God demonstrates His power to overcome their tragic loss and bring good out of evil. He will heal us with His love and enable us to glorify Him and thwart Satan by empowering us to go on because Jesus Christ has defeated our last enemy—death.

By His grace, God has given Edith Schaeffer a wider ministry as a widow than when Fran was alive. To demonstrate the reality of prayer and to show that God is all-sufficient to meet every need, God allowed Fran to die before Edith. And God has shown through her that He can accomplish great things through single or widowed individuals who are devoted to honoring Him.

After Fran died, a friend of L'Abri gave Edith the money to buy a used Steinway baby grand piano in his memory. After Edith found one to buy, she learned about Steinway and traveled to New

York City to research and write her book *Forever Music*. While doing her research at Steinway, she met a master piano technician, Franz Mohr. As a young boy, Mohr lived in Germany during World War II. He suffered many hardships; however, he finally became a Christian after reading Francis Schaeffer's books. With God's perfect timing again, He brough Franz and Edith together. Franz's Christian testimony and ministry to the great pianists so moved Edith that she helped Franz write *My Life With the Great Pianists*. In 1987, Edith worked with the artist, Floyd Hosmer, to create *The Art of Life*. Her book includes more than 30 beautiful pen-and-ink drawings by Hosmer, and devotional readings accompany each piece of art. Since Fran's death, Edith has begun a special ministry to artists and musicians. And she has invited musicians to come to her home and L'Abri to share their talents with others. In addition to helping people from all walks of life, Edith could be called (along with Fran) "a missionary to intellectuals."

After the death of Francis Schaeffer, Edith came forth from serving in the background with a new life and vitality all her own. Intellectually, she is equal to her husband, and still carries on discussions with believers and unbelievers much the same as he did. As a writer, she is more prolific than her husband, and all of her writings apply her husband's innovative approach to philosophical and theological teaching in the practical areas of home and family life. With her autobiographical works, she shows how they lived on the basis of their teachings and how God answered their prayers. When Fran and Edith were married, God blended two lives together in a beautiful way to serve Him; and apart, God has given her the guidance and strength to reach out successfully into new areas of ministry (such as the arts and music).[1]

Edith Schaeffer still prays for those of the Lord's choice to come to L'Abri and for the Lord to provide the food and shelter for those He sends. As she prepares her menus for those coming to dinner, she still prays for God to send His "surprise" guests. She delights in asking each person who knocks on her door, "Well, how did you get here?" because she wants to learn how God has been working in their lives to bring them to L'Abri. She often thanks God immediately for His leading that person to her or to L'Abri. Edith prays for those coming to L'Abri for high tea as she cooks, but she does not pray out of a legalistic compulsion, thinking, "Now I am preparing a menu, so now I must take time to pray for people to come and eat." No, she prays out of love and wonder to a God who will send her people she can serve. She prays for the specific needs of those she knows will be there, because she knows that her prayers will make a difference in each one who comes. She prays that their questions may be answered. And if she is in a group, she prays that people will ask questions that will help others, and that God will give her the needed answers to share. Prayer for others is the natural and supernatural joy of her life, because Jesus is her closest Friend and she maintains a Christlike, servant spirit through Him. Her prayers for others come naturally, because God has implanted His love for us in her heart.

When people talk to Edith on the phone, almost always before they hang up, Edith says, "Let's pray." Whether a local or long-distance call, Edith prays. After 81 years, the life of prayer comes to her so spontaneously that silent and spoken prayers in almost every context make up a large part of her life in addition to her special daily quiet times.[2]

For her quiet times, Edith still reads *Daily Light* each day, and in addition reads through her Bible. She does not skip around, but reads straight through expecting God to speak to her personally by His written Word. She writes notes or prayers to God in her Bible as she prays, and she dates her notes. Over the years, she has written thousands of notes to God through several Bibles. She still prays in the context of a verse, using its words or phrases in praising God or in applying them to her spiritual needs, the needs of L'Abri, and the needs of others.

When Edith prays out loud with others, she praises God and thanks Him especially for the work He has done through Christ in the person's life for whom she is praying. She thanks God for bringing the people of His choice together, and for the work He is now doing in each person's life. She intercedes for any special needs the other person has, and prays for some of the needs of L'Abri, believing that when people unite in prayer God will respond as He has promised. If she receives a letter asking for prayer, she will pray for that person right then as she reads the letter. She does not want to write back "I'll pray for you" and then forget to do so. These are some of the ways God has led Edith to pray as He has taught her over the years, and her prayer life is simply the supernatural outgrowth of her salvation and spiritual life. Though she continues writing and speaking, her praying for others may be her most important work.

The ministry of L'Abri and Edith's continuing ministry is God's answer in the twentieth century to Paul's prayer in the first century. Paul prayed for the Church: "And this is my prayer: that your love may abound more and more in knowledge and depth of insight" (Philippians 1:9). A major purpose in life is loving God and others intelligently, and our prayer requests will reflect love, reason, and faith as we pray and read the Bible. Indeed, as our knowledge and depth of insight increase, our love for God and compassion for others will increase. If not, we are not true believers or our orthodoxy has become cold and sterile.

Most of us have met some who have professed to be highly intelligent and Christian, who have allowed themselves to become puffed up with pride or who have used their intellect to beat down others or make others submit to their heartless doctrines. By the grace of God, Francis and Edith Schaeffer did not succumb to the temptation to use their intellect to build themselves up or tear others down. Through L'Abri, they remained humble servants of all, and their love for others motivated them to build others up in true faith; for this reason they led many skeptical and cynical people to the Savior. By their example, they taught others to pray that increased knowledge would not puff them up, but show them more ways to express the love of God. By their lives, we learn that we can pray to God and God will hear us because He is there. We can pray to God with confidence, because He is not silent: God speaks to us through the Bible. From looking at their lives, we see what God can do through people devoted to following Jesus Christ and the Word of God. May the Holy Spirit move us to work for God with a faith and devotion that He can bless.

Notes

Introduction

1. See "Where to Find L'Abri," p. 143.
2. Edith Schaeffer, *L'Abri* (Wheaton, Ill.: Tyndale House Publishers, 1969), pp. 124–125.
3. See Francis A. Schaeffer, *He Is There and He Is Not Silent* in *The Complete Works of Francis A. Schaeffer: A Christian Worldview*, "A Christian View of Philosophy and Culture" (Westchester, Ill.: Crossway Books, 1982), Volume One, pp. 273–352.
4. A. W. Tozer, *Let My People Go: The Life of Robert A. Jaffray* (Camp Hill, Pa.: Christian Publications, 1990), p. 1.
5. It would have been impossible for me to try to capture Edith's style of writing in this book, and I have not tried. Each writer's style, just as each Christian's prayer life, will be intensely personal. I do encourage you to read Edith's books for yourself, and I hope this book will inspire you to do so.
6. He often said that *True Spirituality* was the most important book he ever wrote and the only one he ever reread to keep in touch with the re-

ality of what he was doing. Francis A. Schaeffer, *True Spirituality* in *The Complete Works of Francis A. Schaeffer: A Christian Worldview*, "A Christian View of Spirituality" (Westchester, Ill.: Crossway Books, 1982), Volume Three, pp. 195–378. See also the important books, *The Church Before the Watching World* and *The Mark of the Christian* in *The Complete Works*, "A Christian View of the Church," Volume Four, pp. 113–205.

7. Dr. Schaeffer died of cancer in Rochester, Minnesota, in 1984. Mrs. Schaeffer still makes her home there and works with the L'Abri branch they founded in Rochester.

Chapter One

1. Edith Schaeffer, *The Tapestry* (Waco, Tex.: Word Books, 1981), p. 52. See also the award-winning special memorial edition in the 1984 paperback.
2. Francis Schaeffer, *The New Super-Spirituality* in *The Complete Works of Francis A. Schaeffer* (Westchester, Ill.: Crossway Books, 1982), Volume Three, Book Three, p. 391.

Chapter Two

1. *The Tapestry,* p. 60.
2. Ibid., 62.

Chapter Three

1. Edith Schaeffer, *L'Abri Family Letters* (July 17, 1984), p. 8.
2. Edith Schaeffer, *Affliction* (Old Tappan, N.J.: Revell, 1978).

Chapter Four

1. Edith Schaeffer, *Christianity Is Jewish* (Wheaton, Ill.: Tyndale House Publishers, 1975).
2. *The Tapestry,* p. 256.
3. Ibid., 258.
4. Ibid., 261.
5. Because of their commitment to these Christian ideals, many young people raised in liberal churches came to them at L'Abri and found faith.
6. See especially Fran's sermon "No Little People, No Little Places" in his book of sermons, *No Little People* in *The Complete Works*, Volume Three, Book One, pp. 5–14.
7. *Two Contents, Two Realities* in *The Complete Works*, Volume Three, Book Four, p. 411.

Chapter Five

1. During the 1980s, Dr. Koop became the United States Surgeon General.
2. You can learn how to buy Prophecy Editions of the New Testament by writing to Million Testaments Campaigns, 1211 Arch Street, Philadelphia, PA, 19107, USA.
3. Edith Schaeffer, *With Love, Edith: The L'Abri Family Letters*, 1948–1960 (San Francisco: Harper & Row, 1988), p. 273.
4. Francis Schaeffer, *Basic Bible Studies* (Wheaton, Ill.: Tyndale House Publishers, 1972). Some people have become Christians in my churches as the direct result of group studies of this book.
5. *True Spirituality* in *The Complete Works*, Volume Three, Book Two, p. 223.

Chapter Six

1. *The Tapestry,* p. 315.
2. *True Spirituality* in *The Complete Works*, Volume Three, Book Two, p. 346.
3. *True Spirituality* became the one book of his that Fran read over again to remind himself of the reality of the Christian faith and of the importance of balance in the Christian life. In *The Church Before the Watching World* in *The Complete Works*, Volume Four, Book Two, Fran gives a historical critique of theological liberalism, and warns against apostasy in the church. He argued that an unbelieving world is watching, so we must rightly represent the love and truth of Jesus Christ before others.
4. *The Tapestry,* p. 356.
5. Ibid., 388.
6. Ibid., 394.

Chapter Seven

1. *The Tapestry,* p. 420.
2. In *The Tapestry*, Edith called this answering prayer "backwards," p. 421.
3. *With Love, Edith,* p. 319.
4. *L'Abri* pp. 15–16. *L'Abri* gives Edith's full and exciting account of the founding of L'Abri and God's many wonderful answers to prayer.
5. Personal conversation with the author.
6. To clarify his views, however, he did add a special appendix on the ways he presented Christian truth in the first volume of his *Complete Works*, pp. 175–187.

Chapter Eight

1. See Dr. and Mrs. Howard Taylor, *J. Hudson Taylor: God's Man in China* (Chicago: Moody Press, 1965). See George Müller, *The Autobiography of George Müller*, edited by H. Lincoln Wayland, (Grand Rapids, Mich.: Baker Book House, 1981, reprinted from the 1861 edition).
2. To write them or any other L'Abri branch, see "Where to Find L'Abri," p.143.

Chapter Nine

1. *The Tapestry,* p. 575. His talk at the Congress was published as *Two Contents, Two Realities.* Dr. Schaeffer was prophetic. Ten years before he wrote *The Great Evangelical Disaster* he warned: "Almost certainly if we have a latitudinarianism in religious cooperation, the next generation will have a latitudinarianism in doctrine, *and especially a weakness toward the Bible.*" *Two Contents, Two Realities* in *The Complete Works*, Volume Three, Book Four, p. 411.
2. In this book I have drawn a distinction between Bible-believing Christians and liberal theologians or "liberal Christians." I am reminded of what a former missionary to Korea, Dick Lash, said to me once after I said, "I am a Bible-believing Christian." He replied, "Can there be any other kind?"
3. This was my experience. For elaboration, see "The Quiet Assurance of Truth" in *Francis A. Schaeffer: Portraits of the Man and His Work*, edited by Lane T. Dennis, (Westchester, Ill.: Crossway Books, 1986).
4. *The Tapestry,* pp. 591–592.

5. *L'Abri Family Letters, The* (December 29, 1973).

Chapter Ten

1. *The Rochester Post-Bulletin,* October 27, 1983, p. 13.
2. *Daily Light on the Daily Path,* from the New International Version, The Zondervan Corporation, 1981.
3. *L'Abri Family Letters, The* (July 17, 1984), p. 9.

Chapter Eleven

1. See especially, Edith Schaeffer, *Forever Music* (Grand Rapids, Mich.: Baker Book House, 1992), and Edith Schaeffer, *The Art of Life,* compiled and edited by L. G. Parkhurst, Jr., (Eastbourne: Kingsway Publicatioins, 1988), and (Wheaton, Ill.: Crossway Books, 1987).
2. See Edith Schaeffer, *The Life of Prayer* (Westchester, Ill.: Crossway Books, 1992.

Where to Find L'Abri

BRITISH L'Abri:
The Manor House,
Greatham, Hampshire
United Kingdom, GU33 6HF
Phone: Blackmoor 436
(Audio tape catalogs available upon request)

DUTCH L'Abri:
Kromme Niewe Gracht 90
3512 HM Utrecht, Holland
Phone: (030) 31 69133

SWEDISH L'Abri:
Per Staffan and Lisa Johansson
Ryggasstugan, Ransvik,
N. Strandvagen 72, 260 42
Molle, Sweden

SWISS L'Abri:
Chalet Bellevue
1861 Huémoz, Switzerland
Phone: (025) 35 21 39

USA L'Abri:
L'Abri Fellowship Foundation
1465 12th Avenue, N.E.
Rochester, Minnesota 55906
Phone: (507) 282 3292

L'Abri Fellowship
49 Lynbrook Road
Southborough, Massachusetts 01772
Phone: (617) 481 6490

The Francis A. Schaeffer Foundation

You may also learn more about Francis and Edith Schaeffer and their continuing influence by writing The Francis A. Schaeffer Foundation, 100 Hardscrabble Road, Braircliff Manor, New York 10510 Phone: (914) 747 9102.

Recommended Reading

Edith Schaeffer, *Affliction* (Old Tappan, N.J.: Fleming
H. Revell Company, 1978). (The latest edition is
with Baker Book House.)

Edith Schaeffer, *The Art of Life*, compiled and edited
by L. G. Parkhurst, Jr., art by Floyd E. Hosmer.
(Wheaton, Ill.: Crossway Books, 1987).

Edith Schaeffer, *Christianity Is Jewish* (Wheaton, Ill.:
Tyndale House Publishers, 1975).

Edith Schaeffer, *Forever Music* (Grand Rapids: Baker
Book House, 1986, 1992).

Edith Schaeffer, *L'Abri* (Wheaton, Ill.: Tyndale House
Publishers, 1969). (The Story of the Founding of
L'Abri.)

Edith Schaeffer, *L'Abri: New Expanded Edition*
(Wheaton, Ill.: Crossway Books, 1992).

Edith Schaeffer, *The Tapestry* (Waco, Tex.: Word
Books, 1981, 1984). (The Schaeffer's Autobiography.)

Edith Schaeffer, *With Love, Edith: The L'Abri Family
Letters, 1948–1960* (San Francisco: Harper & Row,
1988).

Edith Schaeffer, *Dear Family: The L'Abri Family Letters, 1961–1986* (San Francisco: Harper & Row,
1989).

Edith Schaeffer, *The Life Of Prayer* (Wheaton, Ill.: Crossway Books, 1992).

Francis A. Schaeffer, *The Complete Works of Francis A. Schaeffer: A Christian Worldview*, "A Christian View of Philosophy and Culture" (Westchester, Ill.: Crossway Books, 1982). (Includes all 21 of his books in five volumes.)

Francis Schaeffer, *Letters of Francis A. Schaeffer*, edited with introductions by Lane T. Dennis, (Westchester, Ill.: Crossway Books, 1985).

L. G. Parkhurst, Jr., "The Quiet Assurance of Truth" in *Francis A. Schaeffer: Portraits of the Man and His Work*, edited by Lane T. Dennis (Westchester, Ill.: Crossway Books, 1986).

My biography of Francis and Edith Schaeffer contains some material from two of my previous books about them:

L. G. Parkhurst, Jr., *Francis Schaeffer: The Man and His Message* (Wheaton, Ill.: Tyndale House Publishers, 1985). (A brief biographical sketch and interpretation of his theology for laypeople.)

L. G. Parkhurst, Jr., *How God Teaches Us to Pray: Lessons from the lives of Francis and Edith Schaeffer* (Milton Keynes, England: Word Publishing, 1993).

Christopher Catherwood, *Five Evangelical Leaders* (Wheaton, Ill.: Harold Shaw Publishers, 1985).

John D. Woodbridge, editor, *Great Leaders of the Christian Church* (Chicago: Moody Press, 1988).

Acknowledgments

Many people made this book possible. First, I wish to thank Edith Schaeffer for her prayers in its behalf: we pray that it will truly help others. This biography contains only a small slice of the whole, and I hope that after reading it you will want to read Edith Schaeffer's autobiographical books: *L'Abri; The Tapestry; With Love, Edith*; and *Dear Family*. I also wish to thank the Schaeffers and L'Abri for their ministry to me and my family since 1978.

Second, I want to thank Pat, my wife, and Kathryn, my daughter, for their typing and reading of the manuscript and making many helpful suggestions. The book reads better for their efforts. I also want to thank Jonathan, my son, for giving me some helpful insights on the Scriptures as I wrote.

Third, I wish to thank my parents, Gifford and Trudie, for raising me in a Christian home and for being consistent Christian witnesses throughout their lives. Because of their faithfulness, I had a faith "to come back to" after Dr. Schaeffer answered my questions.

Finally, I wish to thank Bethany House Publishers for adding this book to their series WOMEN AND MEN OF FAITH. Bethany House has published many of my books since 1979, and I am grateful to them. I do pray that this will be as helpful as the others in their series.